WITHIN OUR REACH

*The Hoover Institution gratefully acknowledges
the following individuals and foundations for their
significant support of the*

**Initiative
on**
*American Educational Institutions
and Academic Performance*

KORET FOUNDATION
TAD AND DIANNE TAUBE
LYNDE AND HARRY BRADLEY FOUNDATION
BOYD AND JILL SMITH
JACK AND MARY LOIS WHEATLEY
FRANKLIN AND CATHERINE JOHNSON
JERRY AND PATTI HUME
DORIS AND DONALD FISHER
BERNARD LEE SCHWARTZ FOUNDATION
ELIZABETH AND STEPHEN BECHTEL JR. FOUNDATION
CLAYTON AND DOROTHY FRYE

---

*The Hoover Institution
gratefully acknowledges generous support from*

TAD AND DIANNE TAUBE
TAUBE FAMILY FOUNTATION
KORET FOUNDATION

*Founders of the program on
American Institutions and Economic Performance*

And Cornerstone gifts from

SARAH SCAIFE FOUNDATION

WITHIN OUR REACH

How America Can Educate
Every Child

Edited by
John E. Chubb

Published in cooperation with the
HOOVER INSTITUTION
Stanford University • Stanford, California

ROWMAN & LITTLEFIELD PUBLISHERS, INC.
Lanham • New York • Toronto • Oxford

ROWMAN & LITTLEFIELD PUBLISHERS, INC.

The Hoover Institution on War, Revolution and Peace, founded at Stanford University in 1919 by Herbert Hoover, who went on to become the thirty-first president of the United States, is an interdisciplinary research center for advanced study on domestic and international affairs. The views expressed in its publications are entirely those of the authors and do not necessarily reflect the views of the staff, officers, or Board of Overseers of the Hoover Institution.

www.hoover.org

Published in the United States of America
by Rowman & Littlefield Publishers, Inc.
A wholly owned subsidiary of The Rowman & Littlefield Publishing Group, Inc.
4501 Forbes Boulevard, Suite 200, Lanham, Maryland 20706
www.rowmanlittlefield.com

PO Box 317
Oxford
OX2 9RU, UK

Distributed by National Book Network

British Library Cataloguing in Publication Information Available

Library of Congress Cataloging-in-Publication Data

Within our reach : how America can educate every child / edited by John E. Chubb.
    p. cm.
    ISBN 0-7425-4887-2 (cloth : alk. paper) — ISBN 0-7425-4888-0 (pbk. : alk. paper)
    1. Education and state—United States. 2. Education—Aims and objectives—United States. 3. United States. No Child Left Behind Act of 2001. I. Chubb, John E.

    LC89.W59 2005
    379.73—dc22   2005003625

Printed in the United States of America

∞™ The paper used in this publication meets the minimum requirements of American National Standard for Information Sciences—Permanence of Paper for Printed Library Materials, ANSI/NISO Z39.48-1992.

Contents

NCLB
Koret Task Force
Prologue

November 2004

With the reelection of President George W. Bush, it is tempting to think that the future of the nation's most important education law has been secured. No Child Left Behind (NCLB), after all, was the focus of every education debate during the campaign. Senator John F. Kerry and his Democratic allies called for its major overhaul. The president and his supporters staunchly defended NCLB's ambitious ends as well as its controversial means. After a bitter campaign, the president won the popular vote and the electoral vote, and the Republican Party increased its majorities in the Senate and the House. If the president wants to stay the course with NCLB, he can almost certainly have his way.

But if President Bush and Education Secretary–designate Margaret Spellings and their associates choose this course, they will be wasting a rare opportunity. As we show in this study of NCLB, the administration and Congress have a chance to make improvements in the quality of education in America that are desperately needed and potentially historic. NCLB is the most significant federal education initiative since *Brown v. Board of Education* sought to bring equality to America's schools. It is a very good thing for America's students that the overhaul promised by Senator Kerry will not come to pass. That "overhaul," so popular with teachers unions and other establishment critics of the law, would have done nothing more than thoroughly weaken, even cripple NCLB.

Supporters of NCLB—and this includes both many Democrats who voted for it in 2001 and most Republicans—should not rest on their laurels, for the potential of NCLB will not be fully realized if the president chooses simply to stay the course. As we show, the current law does need change—not only to strengthen it but to avoid potentially calamitous problems only now appearing on the horizon. The White House should take advantage of the brief honeymoon that the administration will likely enjoy during the first months of its second term to reform NCLB along the lines that we outline.

The administration may be tempted to delay. NCLB does not have to be reauthorized until 2007. The president has other worthy education initiatives, particularly upgrading high schools and rewarding teachers; calling for midcourse corrections can open the law to mischievous changes by opponents. Yet without the kinds of reforms that we describe, the future reauthorization of NCLB is likely to be conducted in an atmosphere of crisis. Such an environment does not produce the best legislation and, if intense enough, could significantly weaken or even eliminate results-based accountability in American K–12 education.

An ounce of well-timed prevention could do a world of good. Accordingly, the president should use some of his considerable political capital to reach out to those Democrats and Republicans who embrace NCLB's serious purpose, to focus attention on strengthening its functioning, and to agree on important changes that could usher in an era of high achievement, narrowing gaps and creating near-universal proficiency in core academic skills among young Americans.

Executive Summary
Saving NCLB
Koret Task Force

Findings

1. The No Child Left Behind Act (NCLB) has the potential to drive historic improvement in the *quality* of America's schools. Indeed, NCLB could do for the *quality* of America's schools what *Brown v. Board of Education* did for the *equality* of America's schools.
2. Early evidence suggests that NCLB has already spurred significant achievement gains, including a doubling of the rate of improvement in the nation's largest school systems.
3. The potential of NCLB derives from the basic principles that it employs to catalyze change—*accountability, transparency, and choice*—principles that are fundamentally different from the traditional guidelines of public education.
4. There is strong evidence that the kinds of tough accountability measures adopted by NCLB have been raising achievement in states since 1994, and there is reason to believe that the transparency and choice provisions of NCLB can do the same: the law has dramatically increased the visibility of student achievement nationwide and stimulated the entry of many new providers into public education.

5. The major goal of NCLB is audacious: to have all public school students proficient in reading and math by 2014. But this goal is morally right and, we find, attainable; the standards of proficiency adopted by many states, as required by NCLB, reflect levels of performance that are both important for all students to reach and within the grasp of all students, if properly instructed—a judgment that is supported by comparisons of state and national academic standards. The law also provides ample allowance for students in exceptional circumstances—for example, students with serious special education needs or non-English-speaking students newly arrived in the country—to satisfy alternative standards or proceed at a slower pace.

6. Although it is often asserted in the political arena that NCLB is underfunded, and therefore incapable of reaching its goals and hence unreasonable to be expected to, funding should not be at issue. It is a red herring. The direct costs of implementing NCLB's requirements are more than covered by the substantial funding increases that have followed its enactment. The indirect costs are highly debatable, for they are nothing more or less than the costs of public education that states and districts are otherwise expected to provide.

7. The goals of NCLB are nevertheless in serious jeopardy. They will not be reached without modifications to the law (and its administration) *to reinforce the principles on which the law is based* and to strengthen its key processes. NCLB's framers had to accept many compromises to obtain passage in Congress in 2001. Experience now makes clear that those compromises jeopardize the law's major ambition.

8. Our recommendations are unambiguously aimed at helping the law meet its goals according to its demanding timetable. They must not be confused with all-too-frequent calls for "midcourse corrections" by interest groups and policy analysts that would effectively gut NCLB in the name of "feasibility" and "fairness."

9. Despite its promising evidence of progress, NCLB suffers several major weaknesses that threaten its success:

a. States have used the discretion provided them by NCLB to set proficiency standards that vary widely in difficulty (and worthiness), that in some cases have begun to decline, and that are likely to foster a "race to the bottom," driving academic standards further downward as 2014 approaches rather than establishing and sustaining the high standards intended by the law.

b. Some states have used the discretion provided by NCLB to set intermediate proficiency targets (what the law calls annual measurable objectives, or AMOs) that spare most schools from any improvement efforts for several years, delay the need for major achievement gains by all schools for many years, yet promise to cause most schools to be labeled failures later in the decade—an untenable outcome. If this prospective "train wreck" is allowed to happen, the nation will have little alternative but to ignore NCLB or indefinitely delay its implementation.

c. NCLB's mandate that (by 2005–2006) all public school students must be taught by "highly qualified teachers" who are proficient in their subject areas is being satisfied in disingenuous ways that do not in fact ensure that teachers know their content areas. Some states have used their discretion under NCLB to adopt tests for new teachers and alternative requirements for veteran teachers (HOUSSE provisions) that are far too easy. Unless this portion of NCLB is modified, the law will not significantly improve the quality of teachers.

d. The major new engine in NCLB for raising student achievement is choice: the right of students in faltering schools to choose a new school or private tutoring (known as supplementary education services, or SES). These promising strategies for getting students better education are being resisted by the school districts responsible for implementing them. Unless this situation changes, these powerful forces for improvement, equality, and opportunity will fall well short of their potential, leaving NCLB with far less chance of succeeding.

Recommendations

1. *We recommend that all state proficiency standards be calibrated using the National Assessment of Educational Progress (NAEP) as a common yardstick.* The point is to give states that set high standards an incentive to keep them while giving states with low standards an incentive to raise them. We recommend specifically that NAEP be used to rank all states using its rigorous standards and that these rankings be made public. We further recommend that states above the median be given extra time, proportional to their distance from the median, to reach the goal of 100 percent proficiency. States below the median would be encouraged by the public exposure of their low standards to lift theirs.

2. *We recommend that the system of state AMOs, created to evaluate whether schools are making adequate yearly progress (AYP) toward 100 percent proficiency, be replaced by straightforward statistical forecasts of whether individual schools are making adequate progress.* The purpose of this reform: to give all schools immediate incentives to raise student achievement, to avoid drawing misleading conclusions that schools are making adequate yearly progress when they are not, and to resolve issues of how large subgroups must be evaluated for making progress. We recommend using each school's recent and current test scores to project its total and subgroup achievement forward to 2014. Schools that fall significantly below the trajectory needed to reach 100 percent by 2014 would not make AYP and would thus become subject to NCLB's accountability provisions.

3. *We recommend that the definition of highly qualified teacher be revised to include any teacher who possesses a bachelor's degree and one of these three additional attributes: (1) a college major in the subject being taught, (2) passage of a subject competency test provided or approved by an independent national agency on teacher certification, or (3) demonstration through a statistically sound value-added methodology that one's teaching has significantly raised pupil scores on state proficiency tests— thereby eliminating the ineffective HOUSSE provisions of*

NCLB. There is a dual purpose here: first, to attract more promising candidates to teaching by concentrating on skills directly related to student performance and providing alternatives to time-consuming and often ineffective traditional certification; second, to retain effective veteran teachers by focusing directly on their subject matter knowledge and teaching effectiveness and to weed out ineffective ones who are holding down positions better given to new, highly qualified teachers.

4. *We recommend that NCLB take away from school districts primary responsibility for the law's choice provisions and put them in the hands of a state education agency. We further recommend that eligible parents and students be able to choose any regular or charter public school in* any *school district—provided the family handles transportation out of the district—as well as any* private *school that accepts public per capita funding as full tuition. We also recommend that SES services (as well as choice) be available to students whose schools fail to make adequate yearly progress for two consecutive years.* The purpose of these proposals is multifold: transparency, to ensure that the parents know the status of their schools and the alternatives open to them; choice, to increase the probability that students have ample alternatives to select among, should they wish to change schools; and effectiveness, guaranteeing that direct help to students in the form of tutoring from a competent provider is available as soon as possible. This recommendation would also end an unacceptable conflict of interest built into NCLB today whereby a school district is expected to foster alternatives to its own services.

National Goals and Local Control

The key impediment to achieving the bold objectives of the No Child Left Behind Act, objectives that both political parties enthusiastically embraced, is the law's reluctance to interfere with traditional state and local powers and prerogatives. We believe that America's tradition of decentralized primary-secondary education has many virtues. We also believe that important national goals, such as ensuring that every U.S. student reach proficiency, can and should be accomplished through a system that respects state and local control. We would be a poorer nation were this not possible. We strive in this volume to recommend modifications to NCLB that will enable the policy to accomplish what it intended while respecting and maintaining vital state and local roles. The balance between state and nation needs to be altered, yes. But every level of government retains a crucial responsibility in achieving universal proficiency for every young American.

1

Saving No Child Left Behind

John E. Chubb

With the enactment of No Child Left Behind (NCLB) in 2002, the United States may have taken a historic stride toward improving American education. This is a bold prediction, to be sure. But NCLB is not like any federal education law before it, setting ambitious goals for what all students in America will learn and authorizing radical measures to achieve them. In a nation where most students fail to reach proficiency in reading and mathematics and where efforts to raise achievement have fallen short for many years, NCLB mandates that every student in America's public schools will be proficient by 2014—in barely a decade. If schools fail to make sufficient annual progress toward this goal, NCLB holds them strictly accountable: schools are seriously sanctioned and students in those schools are given meaningful alternatives for getting educated—measures that are quite new to public education.

Only two years into the law's implementation, it is already clear that NCLB is breaking educational china—if not a new educational path. More than one in every ten public schools is already facing sanctions for failing to make adequate yearly progress (AYP) at least two years running. Nearly a third are at risk of sanctions, having failed to make AYP once.[1] Public educators have complained loudly about the unfairness of the law. Politicians of both political parties have made NCLB the sole focus of the national education debate. With a newly elected president in Washington, expectations are widespread that NCLB may be revised in 2005, two years before its next scheduled reauthorization.

Modifications are indeed warranted. But the changes that are most necessary are not the ones that have been bandied about in policy circles or recommended by interest groups on Capitol Hill. NCLB currently occupies the moral high ground in education. No one dares oppose its ambitious goals—at least publicly. And so we hear talk about the need for "technical fixes" and "midcourse corrections," reforms ostensibly to preserve the goals but make their attainment fairer or more feasible. The definition of AYP, for example, needs to be relaxed so that "good" schools are not branded as failures. The 2014 timetable needs to be adjusted so that successful schools, at least, can meet it. Or the law needs more funding to match the magnitude of its challenge. These familiar suggestions either miss the point of NCLB or, in effect, aim to undermine its basic purpose. They will not save NCLB; they will gut it.[2]

This is unfortunate because NCLB deserves saving. The law has the potential to improve public education more than any federal education initiative since *Brown vs. Board of Education* over fifty years ago. *Brown* set the historic precedent for *equality* in education; NCLB could set the precedent for *quality*. What distinguishes NCLB from any federal education policy before it is that it is based on fundamentally different principles than those that have historically driven public education. As the nation takes stock of how NCLB is working and how it may need to be reformed, protecting these principles should be the highest priority.

Protecting First Principles

Although No Child Left Behind is now widely viewed as the brainchild of President George W. Bush, it actually has deep roots in federal education policy and the administrations of many presidents, Republican and Democratic alike.[3] Officially, NCLB is a reauthorization of the Elementary and Secondary Education Act (ESEA), first enacted as part of President Lyndon Johnson's Great Society program. The primary aim of ESEA, and especially its largest component, Title I, is to improve the education of students in schools with high levels of poverty by providing supplementary funding. Over the years, ESEA has done very well in adding dollars to economically disadvantaged school districts—providing over 10 percent of the revenue in many—but has done little to improve education. As a result, each reauthorization of ESEA has brought additional regulations aimed at getting more educational bang for Washington's buck. In 1994, when President Clinton used the reauthorization to legislate his Improving America's Schools Act, ESEA added some of the tougher measures found today in NCLB.

Yet for all the reengineering of ESEA, it was plain by the 2000 presidential election that America's schools, and especially its schools serving disadvantaged students, were not raising student achievement fast enough or for enough kids. Both candidates made education a focus of their campaigns, and both emphasized tough new themes: identifying failing schools, using incentives and sanctions to turn them around, holding schools strictly accountable for success, closing schools that do not succeed, and even providing school choice. Although the president hardly won a mandate in the election, both parties had committed to significant change. ESEA became the perfect vehicle to leverage that change, with so many districts dependent on the law's funding.

The change that NCLB sought was like nothing the law had envisioned before. Whereas past versions of ESEA were riddled with loopholes that failing schools slipped through with abandon, NCLB forced change on important new fronts and allowed little room for escape. The law required states to set academic standards and administer annual tests in all schools, not just those receiving Title I funds. It set in stone a demanding national timetable for all students to reach proficiency; past versions of ESEA did not demand proficiency of anyone, let alone in a finite period of time. NCLB also added important new incentives and sanctions to the ones that had failed in the past. Most important, NCLB brought a new set of principles to federal education policy and ESEA. To be sure, these principles were not embraced as fully as they might have been: winning approval of such a major change in policy required significant compromise. Yet these principles undergird NCLB, giving the law unique potential worth protecting.

The first of these principles, obviously enough, is *accountability*. Schools are required to ensure that all their students achieve proficiency in reading and math according to a set schedule or face sanctions. What is important here is that schools are accountable not for *delivering* education to students, the historical norm, but for actually *educating* them—and to high academic standards. Schools are also accountable for ensuring that every student is taught by a teacher who is "highly qualified" to teach his or her subject area. As basic a requirement as this might seem to be, it has never been demanded in America's schools. The second principle is *transparency*. NCLB requires states to make public the scores of every public school on annual assessments for all students and for major economic, racial, ethnic, language, and special educational subgroups. The law provides visibility into school performance that parents, citizens, policymakers, and the media have never had. The third and final principle is *choice*. Students whose schools "need improvement" under NCLB are given the opportunity to transfer to better public schools and to receive tutoring from outside the school system. Disadvantaged students are given a power that middle- and upper-income students have always had: to choose a better school in a different neighborhood (by moving) or to hire a private tutor. NCLB thereby injects an element of the free market into an education system that has been organized strictly on the basis of direct government provision.

As we show in the research collected in this volume, the implementation of these principles through NCLB could make a huge difference for the performance of America's schools. In doing so, NCLB could turn American education in a very different direction, characterized by a sharper focus on results, a more dynamic and responsive system of schools, a place where more able professionals want to work, and, most important, students learning at the high levels that our fast-changing future requires. For this potential to be realized, however, NCLB should not stand pat. Improvements are needed—only not the popular adjustments that, however well meaning, will serve mostly to water down the law. The danger for NCLB is that its principles will be further compromised and the opportunity for major change lost.

In this volume, we take NCLB at its word. The law aims to have all American students reach proficiency within a decade, and it aims to do so by unleashing powerful new forces in education. As we demonstrate, without significant modifications, the law will fall short of changing the way schools operate and improving dramatically what students learn. With reforms, that we detail, NCLB could make a historic difference.

Each chapter collected here examines a major aspect or element of NCLB: historical context and significance; standards and testing; measures of school performance and AYP; accountability systems; sanctions and school improvement; school choice and tutoring; and teacher certification. Each chapter draws on the best available evidence and, except the historical analysis, uses that evidence to judge how a major element of NCLB is working and to suggest what might be done to help it work more effectively. Each chapter should be read for its detailed findings and recommendations. But taken together, the chapters also suggest several broad conclusions. Those conclusions underscore the serious obstacles that NCLB must overcome if it is to make a historic difference and the great potential of the law if meaningful modifications, which we recommend, are undertaken.

Standards and Testing and the Race to the Bottom

One popular line of criticism directed at NCLB has actually been around for some time. *A Nation at Risk*, the 1983 federal report that famously warned of a "rising tide of mediocrity," inspired a rather swift consensus that the nation needed to set higher standards for what students learn. President George H.W. Bush and the fifty governors endorsed the establishment of tough academic standards and the administration of tests for measuring progress toward them in an initiative known as America 2000. President Clinton continued the drive with Goals 2000. Neither initiative came close to reaching its goals, but together they did help move states to adopt, almost universally by the late 1990s, specific standards for what students should know and be able to do and standardized tests to gauge progress. These state initiatives laid much of the groundwork for NCLB—and a major criticism of it: specifically, the imposition of standardized testing and accountability is unfair, biased, and generally detrimental to quality education.

The spread of testing and accountability stimulated a significant backlash, which NCLB must still fight today. Critics attack standardized tests as biased because some racial groups outperform others. Tests are opposed when serious stakes are attached to them, such as receiving a high school diploma. How can a test that requires only a few hours to complete take precedence over years of coursework? The most common criticism is that, as schools try to help students pass their standardized tests, their curriculum becomes narrowly focused on tested skills—often gauged with multiple-choice questions—instead of occupied with the full range of knowledge and skills, such as history, the arts, research, and writing. Testing and accountability, the argument goes, can be the bane of quality education

NCLB has been the target of all of these criticisms. But as we show, these criticisms are largely unfounded.[4] The truth is that NCLB holds state testing to very demanding technical standards. It subjects state tests to a rigorous peer review process free of political bias. It is possible to design tests to measure and thereby reinforce an education that is rich in content and expects students to think at high levels. It is possible to design tests that are in fact free of racial, gender, and other biases. It is feasible to produce tests that reliably gauge student performance with a limited number of items or tasks. Standardized tests can provide an amply valid measure of how well students are mastering almost any standards that states want to set. Most important, NCLB establishes review procedures to ensure that the tests meet these requirements.

One could argue that by requiring only the testing of reading, math, and—in 2007—science, NCLB encourages schools to narrow their curricula to these subjects. But that argument is no more credible than the other criticisms of testing. Reading and math, the only two subjects for which NCLB imposes annual growth targets and requires 100 percent proficiency, are basic to everything else that a student could want to learn. Without proficiency in these subjects students cannot be proficient in any other subject. If a school has to devote more time to these subjects to achieve proficiency, so be it. To do anything else is essentially malpractice. Further, state reading and math standards regularly require that students demonstrate proficiency in ways that are cross-curricular, such as the ability to comprehend scientific and historical texts or the ability to analyze data and use statistics. By asking schools to help all students become proficient in reading and math, NCLB is not narrowing education; it is broadening it—making subjects that would otherwise be inaccessible to the illiterate or innumerate accessible.

Yet there is a problem with standards and testing in NCLB. In deference to the tradition, and perhaps wisdom, of state control over education, NCLB leaves it to the discretion of each state to set its own academic standards, to write its own tests, and to decide for itself what constitutes a proficient score on those tests. The clear expectation of NCLB is that states will set high standards. What is the point of requiring proficiency if proficiency doesn't mean anything? Yet early experience indicates that states have set wildly different standards of proficiency. One way to see this is by comparing the percentages of students proficient on state assessments to the percentages of state students proficient on the federal National Assessment of Educational Progress (NAEP). NAEP sets a high standard, one that only about a third of all students nationwide meet or exceed. Some states, such as South Carolina, have proficiency percentages on their own tests that closely match their percentages on NAEP; other states, such as Texas, have success rates on their homegrown tests that exceed their NAEP performances by more than 40 percentage points. In short, some states have set high standards, others much lower ones.

Differences in standards predate NCLB, but they are likely to be significantly exacerbated by the law. Because NCLB imposes tough sanctions on schools that fail to make adequate yearly progress, states have reason to relax standards, both to protect their schools and to avoid the taint of having large numbers of schools that "need improvement." Already, some states have lowered their standards. Colorado decided to redefine proficiency as "partially proficient" on its state exam. Washington, D.C., dropped its proficiency below the national average to the 40th percentile on the Stanford Achievement Test. Differences in standards have already yielded untenable outcomes, such as Alabama, historically one of the lowest achieving states in the nation, having only 6 percent of its schools with "needs improvement" status while its generally higher achieving neighbor, Florida, has 31 percent.[5] Matters will only get worse as the 2014 deadline approaches and more schools buckle under the weight of rising expectations. Faced with potential levels of failure beyond the national norm, state authorities will be subject to strong local pressure to lower their standards to levels already deemed acceptable by other states. In effect, NCLB could produce a proverbial race to the bottom—states following one another to set progressively lower levels of standards that everyone can live with. NCLB attempts to counter this problem by requiring all states to take NAEP; the U.S. Department of Education can then upbraid states whose own scores are much lower than their NAEP scores. But there is little force in this, and it is already not working. There is a real danger that NCLB could cause educational standards to decline rather than rise.

This problem must be addressed, and we propose a straightforward solution.[6] We believe that NCLB is correct to allow the states to determine what standards and proficiency levels should be. As tempting as it may be to try to solve the problem of declining standards by allowing the federal government to set them for the entire nation, we do not recommend that course. There is no guarantee that the federal government, subject to political pressures of its own, would set high standards. There is also the tradition of state control of education that we see no point in trying to overturn. But there is a way to have one's cake and eat it too—to let states set standards, to encourage those who have set high standards to keep them there, and to avoid a race to the bottom.

We propose a method of benchmarking state standards against the high national standards of NAEP. To simplify, state test scores would be compared with their respective NAEP scores to give states "quasi-NAEP scores." These scores would provide estimates of what state scores would look like if they were graded on the NAEP scale. Each state's proficiency threshold or "cut-point" could also be translated into a quasi-NAEP score. The distribution of these quasi-NAEP proficiency levels would reveal two important pieces of information: what the typical proficiency level is among the states, and how widely individual states vary from what is typical. This information could then be used to encourage states to keep or adjust their standards to reflect what NCLB intended.

Quasi-NAEP scores currently contain some good news along with the bad. The good news is that many states have set proficiency levels that ensure solid reading and math skills. The median state has defined proficiency somewhere between "basic" and "proficient" on the NAEP scale. These NAEP standards, the former being surpassed by about two-thirds of all fourth- and eighth-grade students nationwide and the latter being topped by about a third, are widely regarded as tough definitions of these two levels of achievement.[7] If all states were to settle at least halfway between these two NAEP performance levels, the nation would have academic standards that 50 percent of American students still need to meet—an ambitious goal to be sure—but standards that are not beyond reasonable definitions of grade-level competency, falling short of the NAEP definition of proficiency.

The bad news, however, is that states vary widely around the median, with many—and likely more to come—defining "proficient" as "basic." How can quasi-NAEP measures of state proficiency levels promote higher standards? First, we recommend that any state significantly above the median state proficiency threshold be given more time to achieve the 100 percent proficiency target—the amount of extra time beyond 2014 proportional to the distance the state threshold is above the median. By providing states that have chosen high standards with extra time to reach them, NCLB would give these states incentive to keep their standards high. Second, we recommend that the rank of state standards be updated annually and published in some visible fashion, as a deterrent to states contemplating lowering their standards. The "league tables" used by many countries to rank schools by performance levels could be a model. It is important to note that these recommendations do not represent radical revisions of NCLB. The law already requires all states to take the NAEP and intends the NAEP to serve as a check on state standards. Our recommendations simply extend the idea of requiring NAEP, to give the idea more force. Our proposal should discourage egregious negative deviations from national norms and encourage quality-conscious states to stay the course. NCLB could be the law that finally induces the nation to adopt high standards in all public schools—but not without changes that prevent it from doing exactly the opposite.

Accountability and Sanctions and the Train Wreck Waiting to Happen

Once high standards have been established, it is essential that schools somehow be held responsible for achieving them. This is the other half of meaningful accountability. Schools have administered standardized tests to students for years, but for most of the history of standardized testing, the process has had little systematic impact on the quality of schooling. Indeed, one need go back no more than ten years to find the prevailing view of test scores to be a measure of students, not of schools. But that has changed, and quite dramatically, since the early 1990s. When NCLB was passed, every state in the nation already had standards, testing, and some level of expectations that schools would measure up. Even though these "accountability systems" have been around for barely a decade, there is already strong evidence that they have been a significant plus for student achievement.

The most comprehensive and up-to-date analysis of state accountability systems and their impact on achievement, reported in this volume, provides compelling evidence.[8] This is critically important information for evaluating NCLB because the federal law itself is too new to judge its consequences. Economist Eric Hanushek looks at the improvement in state scores on NAEP as students moved from grade four to grade eight over two intervals, 1994–1998 and 1998–2002. Because states adopted accountability systems at different points in time across these intervals, it is possible to look at achievement growth in states with and without accountability systems. It turns out that achievement growth was significantly higher in states that had accountability systems in place than in those that did not. As important, the difference in achievement only held if the state accountability system had *consequences*, that is, rewards and sanctions, for improving test scores. States that set standards and imposed tests, but did not make schools responsible for their scores did not perform significantly better than schools that did not have standards or tests.

There is an important lesson in these findings for NCLB. The law has the potential to drive achievement nationwide precisely because it requires all states to have standards and tests *and* to hold their schools accountable for making progress. The major challenge is providing accountability. Without accountability, the law would be nothing—much like ESEA had been for generations. But ensuring accountability is not easy. NCLB raises several major concerns; one is what we call the train wreck waiting to happen.

NCLB is anchored by the requirement that all public schools achieve 100 percent proficiency by 2014. To attain such proficiency, states are required to establish interim benchmarks called annual measurable objectives (AMOs) in reading and math. Schools must hit these AMOs each year or reduce their percentages of nonproficient students by 10 percent—the so-called safe harbor provision—or face sanctions. Schools must do this for all tested students and for all subgroups of students of a significant size with high test-participation rates. Schools must also satisfy one other "academic indicator" chosen by their state. Attaining AMOs, satisfying safe harbor requirements, and meeting the other academic indicators are required to make adequate yearly progress (AYP). If schools fail to make AYP in one year, they are put on notice that they are at risk of sanctions. If they fail a second year, they are classified as needing improvement; students in those schools that are also Title I schools are permitted to transfer to another public school (thus exercising choice). A third year of failure makes low-income students in Title I schools eligible for private tutoring—known as supplementary education services (SES). A fourth year changes a school's status to needing corrective action, which requires one of six prescribed major reforms including new curriculum, outside consulting, or new personnel. Year five of failure requires planning for restructuring, through such means as chartering or privatization. Year six requires the execution of restructuring plans.

Several problems with this accountability plan give it little chance for success. One problem is the inadequacy of its choice and SES provisions, which we will address subsequently. The others we turn to now. First, there is little reason to believe that the sanctions aimed at turning failing schools around will do so fast enough to meet the 2014 deadlines—if at all. NCLB permits schools to fail for three years before requiring corrective action, years that are already a large portion of the time that schools have to achieve proficiency before 2014. After failing for a fourth year, NCLB mandates that schools adopt one reform from a menu of major interventions, but there is little evidence that those corrective actions will work. The odds are that many if not most schools will get to the restructuring level of sanctions having squandered six years of precious time available to reach proficiency.

In this volume we present a sobering case study of one of the nation's largest efforts to turn failing schools around.[9] In the late 1990s California began implementing a turnaround program called Immediate Intervention/Underperforming Schools (II/UPS). The program targeted schools that had made the least progress on the state's accountability measure, the academic performance index (API). It asked those schools to employ outside consulting or study teams to help identify reforms that would help schools overcome their chronic failures, and it provided grants to facilitate the process. The II/UPS reads much like the corrective action plans of NCLB. From 1999–2003, hundreds of California schools went through this study and reform process.

According to independent evaluations, the impact on student achievement was negligible. This was because the study teams—representing universities, professional development organizations, independent educational consultants, regional education offices, and the like—came up with a hodge-podge of recommendations that tended to focus more on how schools are organized and operate than on what schools teach and how effectively they teach it. The result was that schools that could not help students master California's tough academic standards before the intervention mostly could not after the intervention.

Thus in 2001 California created a new program for failing schools, the High Priority Schools Grant Program (HPSGP) supported by state School Assistance and Intervention Teams (SAIT). This laser-like effort focused on reading and math achievement, in contrast to the scattershot approach of II/UPS. The methods employed by the SAIT revolve around aligning school curricula with state standards and the successful teaching of those standards. Although it is too early to know with certainty how this new program is working, early reports are encouraging. The difference appears to be its concentration on the educational standards that are the primary measure of school success or failure. The lesson for NCLB is that its open-ended approach to corrective action—a nod again to state control and discretion—is likely to yield a lot of false starts and disappointments when time is of the essence. California, moreover, is only one example of many state intervention efforts that have come up short.

So we wonder whether the six-year cycle of sanctions in NCLB will be able to spur failing schools to full proficiency by 2014. But we are even more concerned about NCLB's accountability provisions—what we term the train wreck waiting to happen. NCLB gives the states considerable flexibility in setting the AMOs that schools must meet on their way to 100 percent proficiency. The law requires that the first AMOs, those for 2002–2003, be set no lower than the proficiency level of the school at the 20th percentile of the statewide proficiency distribution or the proficiency level of the lowest state subgroup, whichever is higher. The provision enables states to begin the trek to 100 percent at low levels. (In a number of states schools can initially make AYP by having less than a fifth of their students proficient.) The law then requires that AMOs increase in equal increments through 2014 but permits them to remain level along the way for up to three years. Thus many states have created a series of steep stair steps two to three years wide that delay much of the progress toward 100 percent until the years just before 2014.

There are many issues with the timetables that states have adopted. One is that schools with proficiency levels above the current AMOs are not required to make any improvement at all. It remains an article of faith that when their time to improve comes along, they will know how to do so. Another is that there is no evidence that schools will be able to accelerate their achievement growth to clear the hurdles that states periodically raise to higher levels. Keeping AMOs at the same level for three years only gives schools a false sense of confidence—they are making AYP—when they should be working to make continuous improvement. Further, there is little evidence to suggest that the current regime of AMOs is producing the kinds of gains that are necessary to reach 100 percent by 2014.

The best evidence of how the AMOs and related accountability measures are working comes from the nation's largest school districts. Urban school systems such as New York, Los Angeles, and Chicago—the three largest—and major county schools systems such as those in the South are the prime targets of NCLB because they educate large numbers of economically disadvantaged students. To see how NCLB may be affecting their performance, we looked at their achievement records over the last two years for which data are complete. In 2001–2002, the baseline year of NCLB, the fifty largest school systems raised their rates of reading and math proficiency by 1.34 and 2.03 percentage points, respectively—an average of 1.46 points overall—on their state tests. In 2002–2003, the first year of NCLB accountability, the fifty largest districts raised reading and math achievement by 2.58 and 2.48 percentage points, respectively—an average of 2.49 points overall.[10] The good news in these figures is that NCLB has been associated with a clear increase in the rate of achievement growth in large school districts. The Council of Great City Schools, which represents many of these districts, has publicly attributed their recent improvement to NCLB.[11] The bad news is that annual achievement gains of two to three points simply will not get the job done. In ten years, districts moving at the latest known rate of gain will improve their proficiency levels by 25 percentage points—important progress to be sure but not enough to get close to 100 percent proficiency, given the low levels that most failing schools are starting with.

The serious problem, then, is that with AMOs not requiring the largest gains for many years, with better schools not being asked to make any improvement at all, and with actual rates of improvement that promise not to reach 100 percent, the accountability timetable will not be met. But more than that, the timetable will not be breached gradually but broken in a massive failure several years down the road, when AMOs suddenly shoot up and all or most schools find themselves sorely challenged to meet them (the train wreck waiting to happen). When this occurs, the federal government will have little choice but to ignore the law or delay its implementation indefinitely. It is simply untenable for the country's public school systems to deal suddenly with the majority of their schools being in official need of improvement.

We believe that this calamity can and should be avoided so that NCLB can fulfill the potential that it clearly has. The answer, we believe, is to rethink the concept of AMOs. The purpose of AMOs is to establish benchmarks with which schools can be held accountable for their progress along the way to 2014. But, as we have shown, because the AMOs are allowed to be set in ways that do not promise to get schools to full proficiency, they should be fundamentally changed. Our new method for evaluating whether schools are *truly* making adequate yearly progress requires no new data, respects the basic goal of NCLB to have all students reach a reasonable level of proficiency, and supports the goal that students from major subgroups should reach proficiency as well.[12]

We propose reconceptualizing AYP as a statistically valid forecast of whether a school and its subgroups are on track to reach 100 percent proficiency by 2014. The progress of each school and its respective subgroups would be evaluated with a statistical model that looked at current year scores along with scores from the school's recent past to estimate where the school will be in 2014 if current trends continue. If a school's trajectory projects to a level that differs from 100 percent in 2014 by a statistically significant amount, the school would not be considered to have made AYP. To begin with, a test of statistical significance would be applied to the school overall and to its subgroups. The same test would be applied at the finish line as well, thus determining whether a school and its subgroups had reached 100 percent with reasonable statistical confidence.

This approach has many virtues. One, it affects all schools immediately, meaning that the many schools above current AMOs would need to begin making progress, as well as those below. Two, it does not rely on arbitrary benchmarks or, worse, benchmarks that reflect wishful thinking about future gains, meaning that the schools must begin to produce ongoing empirical evidence that they can get the job done. Schools cannot hide behind AMOs that do not create immediate challenges. Third, the model puts to rest arguments about how large a subgroup must be to count. States differ arbitrarily in defining the size of meaningful subgroups; our model leaves the impact of the subgroups on AYP to an objective test of statistical significance. The model can even be used to correct for participation rates—another hotly debated issue—if nonparticipants are entered into the model as a minimum score. Statistics can determine when a low participation rate calls into question a school's true progress.

The main virtue of our approach is that it tells us immediately and objectively, based strictly on the evidence, what each school is forecast to achieve in the future. This information will allow every school and school system to begin working promptly, with a full decade to meet the challenges of the law. This goal could also be accomplished in other ways. For example, the progress of individual students might be tracked and schools held accountable for their growth along the entire performance scale—not just clearing the proficiency bar. This would make all schools responsible for achievement gains immediately. Chapter 5 describes such an alternative. Such value-added approaches to accountability, however, require better data systems than many states currently have. They also implicitly ask for a change in the goals of NCLB, from universal proficiency to individual achievement growth. Although recognizing the wisdom of alternate goals and methodologies, we believe it is most urgent—and most feasible—to support the goals of NCLB as adopted. By replacing artificial AMOs with realistic forecasts, NCLB could help schools and states thoughtfully plan for how to reach its tough goals ten years down the road.

Highly Qualified Teachers and the Problem of Top-Down Control

Although NCLB has attracted the most attention for establishing unprecedented accountability for student achievement, the law is no less radical in establishing another important form of accountability—for teachers. For the first time in history, the federal government is saying who can teach in public schools. Heretofore entirely a state prerogative, teacher qualifications are now being specified from Washington. Whatever one may think of the requirements that NCLB imposes, any initiative that is serious about raising student achievement—which NCLB clearly is—must address the quality of teachers. Research has shown beyond doubt that the quality of the teacher in front of the classroom is the most important determinant of what students learn (except for the quality of students themselves). Indeed, a student working with an exceptionally strong or weak teacher for only two consecutive years can be expected to move up or down the national achievement distribution at least two full quartiles. That is potentially life-changing movement, all a result of the quality of the teacher.[13]

NCLB requires schools by 2005–2006 to have every core academic subject taught by a highly qualified teacher (HQT). (It also required all newly hired teachers in Title I schools to be highly qualified by 2002–2003.) The definition of a HQT is very specific: such teachers must hold a bachelor's degree, be certified to teach by their state, and—this is what is new—be competent in their subject area. Newly hired teachers must demonstrate subject-area competence by having a college major in the subject or by passing a subject competency test. Veteran teachers, who have until 2005–2006 to be highly qualified, can do so with a major or a test, but they may also pass muster by satisfying requirements that the law calls "high objective uniform state standards of evaluation" (HOUSSE), which the states have had to set. The requirement of subject competence is what is important here, as states have already insisted on bachelor's degrees and state certification for most teachers. Demonstrated subject competence is what is lacking. A full 78 percent of all public school teachers do not have college majors in the subjects they teach (they largely were education majors), and only half of all secondary teachers—where teachers specialize in particular subjects—have the appropriate subject major. This is important because research also shows that teachers who majored in their subject area are more successful than those who did not.[14]

NCLB takes several steps to ensure that its HQT requirements are carried out. One relies on transparency. Beginning in 2003–2004, schools are required to notify parents of any core academic teachers instructing their children who are not highly qualified. The U.S. Department of Education holds the authority to approve state testing and HOUSSE provisions. Schools receiving Title I funds can have those funds withheld if they fail to have highly qualified faculties. On paper NCLB has the potential to do enormous good for the quality of teaching.

As reported in chapter 7, however, the law is not living up to its potential. The reasons are many. State and district record keeping on teacher education and credentials is poor to uneven, making it difficult for the U.S. Department of Education to verify claims about compliance. A U.S. Government Accounting Office study in July 2003 concluded that the data on teacher qualifications were unreliable. In the fall of 2003, thirty-one states reported that they had at least 80 percent HQT, and 20 states claimed to have at least 90 percent HQT. Among forty-one states that were able to separate schools by level of economic disadvantage, thirty-one reported that their disadvantaged schools were within 5 percent of HQT for the entire state. These high figures, especially for economically disadvantaged schools, do not square with most perceptions of the quality of the teaching force. The Education Trust, an advocacy group for disadvantaged students and a staunch defender of NCLB, responded that these optimistic reports on HQT were not to be believed.

If the numbers seem high, it is most likely because the standards adopted by states to implement HQT are low. NCLB leaves it to the states to create subject competency tests; more important, because it affects some three million veteran teachers, states are also in charge of setting HOUSSE requirements. As Moe demonstrates, most states use this provision to make it as easy as possible for veteran teachers to demonstrate their competence. Teachers can satisfy HOUSSE requirements in the same way that they have always been able to satisfy certification requirements: completing courses, taking professional development seminars, assembling portfolios of work, and other very indirect and unreliable measures of quality. The states have for all practical purposes grandfathered all veteran teachers into the HQT system; few if any veteran teachers will be deemed not highly qualified.

Why has the implementation of this well-intentioned provision of NCLB resulted in messy data, undemanding tests, and the HOUSSE provisions a giant loophole? It is for the very same reason that teacher certification has never been an effective guarantor of teacher quality. HOUSSE requirements, like all certification requirements, are set through the political process—some combination of legislative action and administrative rule making—that is inevitably influenced by the groups with the most intense interest in their outcome and the most resources to throw at them. When it comes to teacher certification, those groups are, first and foremost, teachers unions and, second, college and university schools of education that use the political process to try to create a certification system that meets their needs. Traditionally, this has meant not requiring teachers to have much subject-area knowledge, placing a premium on education courses or majors, and avoiding any formal tests of competence. It has also meant very definitely opposing any effort to impose new requirements on teachers already certified and teaching. In the same way that the political process has long given us ineffectual teacher certification requirements, it has now given us weak HQT requirements, especially for veteran teachers.

Education is hardly unique in the way politics is working. Groups with intense interests in a subject often exert more influence than the general or public interest, which is far more diffuse. Regulated industries, for example, are often said to "capture" the regulatory agencies that oversee them. There is one difference with schools, however. Teachers unions, which dominate school politics, have more financial resources than any interest group in all of state politics, making them an unusually formidable foe if school reforms are not to their liking. The nation's major teachers unions, the National Education Association and the American Federation of Teachers, oppose NCLB (the former being against it outright and the latter wanting it watered down so thoroughly that they may as well be opposed). At the national level, a newly elected President Bush and a bipartisan majority in Congress managed to pass NCLB, over union objections, though with some clear concessions to their Democratic supporters. But once implementing the law moved to the state level, the traditional distribution of power, strongly favoring unions and education schools, took over, with the result that HQT requirements were compromised.

There is a lesson here about school reforms that try to improve schools from the top down. The history of education reform is largely a story of attempting to make schools better by specifying how they should go about their business: what textbooks should be used, how many minutes to devote to each subject, how large classes must be, what programs can be paid for with federal money, and, of course, what certification requirements teachers must satisfy. None of these efforts has been successful because it is difficult to improve educational results by mandating educational processes. Results are best when educators take responsibility for them, when they do not operate simply by following someone else's rules. Reforms have also been disappointing because rules and regulations are heavily influenced by the groups that are least interested in change. These problems, which are inherent in the top-down control of education, are also why policymakers have increasingly favored trying to improve schools by requiring accountability for outcomes, such as student achievement, rather than accountability for process.

Unfortunately, the HQT provisions of NCLB have fallen victim to the politics of top-down control. As desirable as it is to have teachers knowledgeable about their subject areas, and as bold as NCLB is in pursuing this end, the reform is not working—or at least not working well. Yet improving the quality of the teaching force remains critical to improving the quality of public schools. As Moe details, we need to attract stronger candidates to teaching; public school teachers currently come from the low end of the college achievement distribution. This contrasts with private school teachers, who have higher achievement scores—a difference attributable in part to the absence of certification requirements for private schools. State certification requirements, with their time-consuming demands for education coursework (of little demonstrated value) are a deterrent to potential teachers. We therefore recommend a very different approach to improving teacher quality, one that relies less on top-down control, not more.

Specifically, we urge a revision of NCLB to permit individuals with a bachelor's degree, plus one of three straightforward additional qualifications, to be able to teach in any public school in the country. The three additional qualifications—aimed at ensuring subject matter competence in the subject that a teacher teaches—include: (1) a college major in the core subject that the teacher teaches, (2) a passing grade on a subject matter competency test produced or approved by an independent national commission responsible for teacher subject-area competence, and (3) evidence of improved student achievement from teaching a subject area as measured by state proficiency tests and evaluated by a standard value-added methodology. (The third option would obviously only be available for veteran teachers, who could also use options one or two if they preferred.) Under this proposed revision of NCLB, schools would not be able to require additional teacher certification—though universities are obviously free to offer it, if teachers find it valuable.

The logic of these proposals is simple and compelling, we believe. By reducing the initial hurdle to teaching to a bachelor's degree and a college major or competency test, NCLB could sharply increase the supply of new and potentially good teachers. Prospective teachers would not have to take a fifth year of college to complete education courses or decide that they want to teach early in their college career. Prospects could graduate with a passion for their major and decide to try to teach it. With subject-area competence governed by college majors or by tests approved or created at the national level—where traditional interests cannot as easily water down the requirement—new teachers should be not only more plentiful but better prepared to teach than they are today. The biggest difference that NCLB could make is for veteran teachers. By replacing the weak HOUSSE provisions with meaningful measures of competence, NCLB could weed out those teachers for whom there is no evidence that they can succeed or have succeeded. Should some veteran teachers be forced to leave teaching because of this provision, their places would be filled by new recruits who are better qualified.

Choice and Tutoring and the Conflict of Interest

Perhaps the most radical element of NCLB—at least potentially—is its introduction of choice and competition into federal school improvement efforts. Since the early 1990s the nation has been moving slowly toward a model of education that is not controlled exclusively by local school districts, that allows other providers to offer public education, that affords parents more choice over where their children attend school (without changing residence), and that injects a measure of competition into schooling. Although the country is a long way from the reality, the model holds open the possibility that the supply of public schools could become much more dynamic, with unsuccessful schools closing, successful schools replicating, and new schools opening—all much more rapidly than in the traditional district model. Quality should improve more rapidly as well, with parents rejecting schools with poor test scores and embracing schools with good ones. Choice and competition have come to public education in several ways. Some forty states have authorized public charter schools, and roughly three thousand charters serving more than 600,000 students were open in 2004. Several states and the District of Columbia have established voucher programs so that low-income or special education students can attend private schools at public expense, and in 2002 the Supreme Court ruled that such programs could include religious schools. Many states and districts permit parents to choose among public schools—though the choices rarely have the effect of driving unsuccessful schools out of business. NCLB builds on this experience but tries to advance it substantially.

For the first time, federal education policy is trying to drive improvement by going directly to families. NCLB says, in effect, if federal law and the efforts of public educators are unsuccessful in improving a school, the student need not wait for things to get better. If the school does not improve, the student can seek education elsewhere. If a Title I school fails to make AYP two years in a row, the student may choose another district (regular or charter) school that has made AYP, and the district must pay for transportation. If the school fails three years in a row, the student is eligible for tutoring (supplementary education services—SES) from any state-approved provider, including private companies. The district must reserve 20 percent of its Title I funds to pay for choice and SES.

There is great potential in these provisions. The threatened loss of Title I funds—even though Title I appropriations were increased by more than 20 percent to pass NCLB—should make districts work harder to improve their Title I schools and hold onto their funding. Students' transferring out of failing public schools ought to accelerate those schools' closure or reconstitution. Admitting private for-profit and not-for-profit organizations into mainstream public education, albeit as tutors, sets an important precedent for a more competitive supply of instruction. The use of choice and competition by NCLB, then, may have two important consequences. One, it may accelerate the achievement gains of disadvantaged students in Title I schools. Two, it may speed the spread of a new model of public education based more on market principles and less on principles of top-down control.

Thus far, however, the consequences have been minimal. The choice provisions of NCLB have been especially inconsequential. In chapter 8 we look at the latest data on choice and SES.[15] The bottom line on choice is that, despite the large number of schools nationwide that have failed to make AYP two years in a row and officially need improvement, few families and students have elected to leave failing schools. Peterson estimates that in 2003–2004, the second year in which NCLB made choice available, no more than 2 percent of all eligible students transferred. Although this percentage may have been double the meager percentage of the first year of the program, it is well below its potential level.

Surveys indicate that the problem is not that parents or students are satisfied with their low- performing schools. Policy debates often feature the claim that school choice is unlikely to drive school improvement because parents and students are overwhelmingly satisfied with their schools. But although it is indeed true that most parents like their children's schools—two-thirds of parents annually surveyed by Gallup give their school an A or B grade—it is not true that parents in low-performing schools like theirs. Parents with children in schools that failed to make AYP are twice as likely to rate their children's school a C, D, or F than are parents with children in schools that made AYP. Further, parents in failing schools indicate that they want to choose an alternative; nearly half would like a private school, whereas a quarter to a fifth would like another school in the district, a school in a different district, or a charter school. These percentages are well above the actual level of choices being made; thus, the paucity of transfers seems not to be due to parental satisfaction with the status quo.

Rather, local authorities' implementation of NCLB seems to be to blame. School districts are understandably reluctant to encourage mass transfers among their schools. Transfers could leave many buildings half full and others bursting at the seams—because NCLB does not accept capacity as an excuse for denying transfers. Transfers mean reassigning staff, moving books and instructional supplies, wasting facility space, and other inefficiencies, if achievement is left out of the equation.

Transfers can also cost money in increased transportation if students leave neighborhood schools. This is money that districts would rather spend on other programs—and could spend were it not for the exercise of choice. Schools may also be unenthusiastic about choice, fearing that they may lose their best students—making AYP an even tougher target—and, of course, finding themselves with fewer resources. The schools being chosen worry that weaker students may transfer in, hurting their AYP prospects, and bringing insufficient resources. With little incentive to promote choice, districts have complied with the law only minimally, frequently notifying parents of their right to choose late in the summer or even after the school year has begun, when families are least likely to make a change. Letters to parents frequently say kind things about the failing school, assuring parents that staying put is not a bad choice. Districts have also successfully declared eligible receiving schools at capacity, despite regulations that are supposed to make that a rarity.

Compounding the problem of district cooperation are weaknesses in the law itself. Parents may not choose any school that did not make AYP—even if some schools that did not make AYP are far better than others that also did not. Students may not transfer across district lines, unless a receiving school approves—which they have not done very frequently. Of course, students may not choose private schools; this option was proposed for NCLB by President Bush but quickly dropped in the search for a legislative majority. Because the law effectively limits choices to public schools (including charter schools) making AYP within the same district, many school districts have few choices to offer families.

We recommend the following practical solutions to these problems. Families should be eligible to transfer the year after they are notified that their child's school has failed to make AYP—not forced to make a spur-of-the-moment decision. Students should be able to transfer to schools that have not made AYP as well as those that have; not all failing schools have the same difficulties. Students should be able to choose schools across district lines, providing they can come up with transportation. Students should be able to choose private schools, provided those schools will accept government vouchers for the full cost of tuition.

Those measures would make choice more widespread, but they are not what is most needed. Choice under NCLB is lagging because at every turn school districts do not have the incentives to make it work. Therefore, we recommend that states give the oversight of the NCLB choice provisions to an agency independent of the local school districts. That agency's job would be to inform parents about failing schools, provide comprehensive information about the choices available to them, and assist them with requesting and receiving transfers. The basic problem with the choice provision of NCLB is that it leaves implementation responsibility with school districts, which have a fundamental conflict of interest. This above all else must change.

The experience with SES is similar but not nearly as discouraging. In its second year of implementation, SES served about 113,000 students nationally, according to estimates by Peterson. Disadvantaged students in schools that fail to make AYP for three consecutive years are eligible for SES. Because of AYP failures under the ESEA, the predecessor to NCLB, many schools were failing for the third year during the first year of NCLB. Thus it appears that SES was provided to as many as 5 percent of all eligible students and is forecast to keep growing—a different picture from that of choice, certainly. The market for choice has also attracted more than a thousand providers approved by state authorities. Some of the country's largest and most respected tutoring firms, such as Sylvan (now Catapult) Learning, Princeton Review, and Stanley Kaplan, have become significant providers. Other major education companies, such as Edison Schools (through its Newton Learning division), are also participating in big ways. It is too early to tell how student achievement will benefit from this extra instruction. But analogous efforts are routine in other countries and are credited with boosting achievement, the "cram" schools of Japan being the prime example.

The rapid growth of tutoring services, as compared to school choice opportunities, has much to do with differences in supply. NCLB has made roughly a million families eligible for choice and somewhat fewer for SES, creating ample potential demand. But for choice, the only source of supply is under the control of the local school district. For SES, the supply is determined by the private market, which has stimulated more than a thousand organizations to provide what families want. The dramatic response of the private market to the SES opportunity indicates how dynamic the supply of education can be and the likelihood of continued growth in the quantity and quality of SES services.

But SES services could be much better and more extensive than they currently are. Again, the main obstacle is the local school district. As with choice, districts would rather that the enrollment not be large for Title I funds not spent on SES are available to the district for other purposes. Thus, districts have been slow to promote SES with families. Yet an additional problem is that districts are permitted to be SES providers themselves, competing with private providers. In fact, most SES services are currently provided by school districts. Is this because districts do the best tutoring? Perhaps—though eligible schools have failed on their watch. The more straightforward explanation is that districts have an unfair competitive advantage over private providers. Districts control school facilities where tutoring can most easily be done. Districts have access to parents and students—to advertise and recruit—that private organizations do not. Districts have considerable say over which private organizations have the opportunity to compete to be SES providers.

It is clearly a conflict of interest for districts to be both providers of SES and gatekeepers for its provision. Our primary recommendation for improving SES is therefore much the same as for choice. The state should create an independent agency whose job it is to inform parents of SES eligibility, provide parents with comprehensive information about the qualifications and programs of providers, and, finally, offer providers the information and opportunities that they need to reach eligible families. If districts are going to be SES providers, they cannot also be SES regulators; that role should be assigned to a disinterested third party.

One additional recommendation of great import is that because tutoring provides the most immediate support for students who are struggling and because the market has responded so substantially to the demand for tutoring, NCLB should make students eligible for SES the same year they are eligible for choice—after two consecutive years of a school failing to make AYP. That move would accelerate services to needy students and also make public education a more dynamic service allowing it to draw promptly on support from the market.

National Goals and Local Control

In the end, the challenge that faces NCLB—if it is to invoke major improvements in America's schools—is resolving the tension between national goals and local control. With NCLB, for the first time in the nation's history, the federal government is saying that every child, regardless of where they live or what their background is, will be educated to a level of meaningful proficiency. This commitment is every bit as significant as the one made in *Brown* more than half a century ago. Whereas *Brown* promised equality without question, NCLB promises quality. But much as the promise of Brown has proven difficult to fulfill, so too will the promise of NCLB remain elusive—unless the fundamental challenges to it are confronted.

The U.S. Constitution reserves the task of education to the states, and by tradition the federal division of labor has pretty much left it that way. Local school districts remain the public authorities most responsible for the operation of public schools, and the states pay the largest share of public school costs. But since the days of *Brown*, the federal government has steadily increased its role in public education, becoming the leading advocate for equality—for racial minorities, special education students, English language learners, and girls—and has increased its share of public school costs, particularly in needy districts. As the federal role has increased, it has always had to carefully share the stage with states and local districts, which want their historical prerogatives and powers protected. This sharing of power has not made the accomplishment of national goals easy—as the slow and geographically uneven extension of racial equality has proven. Of course, power sharing is what federalism is all about. There can be great benefit, especially in a nation as large and diverse as the United States, to allowing policies to be set differently from place to place.

But there seems to be little debate, at least in this new century, about the desirability of equal and high-quality education regardless of where in the United States a child lives. Public opinion polls show strong support for national education goals. There is no reason to believe that students need to read less well or be less competent in math in one state than another. As we have said, No Child Left Behind occupies the moral high ground. Yet, as we have shown, the law faces serious impediments to its success that have grown almost entirely out of concessions that the law made to the tradition of state and local control.

NCLB asks each state to set the high academic standards that students will meet. That discretion may well cause standards to drop. The law allows states to set the benchmarks that schools will meet on their way to achieving 100 percent proficiency; the states have responded with AMOs that disguise problems in the short term and promise disaster down the road. NCLB asks the states to set subject matter competency standards for teachers; the response has been little more rigorous than the ineffectual certification standards that the states have produced for years. The law asks school districts to offer choice and tutoring to students in failing schools; school districts have followed through reluctantly and inadequately.

The essence of the problem, then, is that NCLB has summoned the national courage to take a bold stand for educational quality but has not mustered similar courage to get the job done. The good news, as we have shown, is that the law is based on sound principles and that those principles can be made to work. *Accountability* is a powerful tool for leveraging school improvement. It has already made a significant difference in states that have adopted it with consequences. NCLB has set the right goal: proficiency for all students by 2014. For this goal to remain meaningful and be reached, however, NCLB must be reformed.

States need to be given incentives to keep their standards high, which can be done, as we have shown, without denying states the power to set those standards. It requires only that state standards be judged against NAEP, as the law already provides, and that states with significantly higher standards be given more time to meet the 100 percent objective. States also need to be required to evaluate the growth of achievement in their schools realistically. The system of AMOs is a train wreck that everyone can see coming. NCLB should replace this system with a sound statistical approach in which adequate yearly progress is based on scientific forecasts for schools and their subgroups. Forecasting would hold all schools accountable for improving right now (while 2014 is still many years away), instead of putting the onus only on schools close to today's low AMOs. Strengthening accountability in these ways, moreover, does little to interfere with important state prerogatives—the states continue to control their standards—but does much to improve NCLB's prospects for success.

With teacher accountability, however, the states cannot be trusted to provide effective teacher quality. The HQT provision of NCLB is not working. But the answer is not to try to control or influence the state regulation of who gets to teach. It is to ban restrictive state certification and replace it with simple qualifications to teach in a public school: a bachelor's degree and one of three demonstrated areas of subject competence—a college major, a passing grade on a nationally approved or developed test, or evidence of improved student achievement on state proficiency tests. If the federal government wants to ensure any quality control in teaching, it should limit itself, as we recommend, to setting standards for teacher content knowledge—the focus of NCLB in the first place. None of these changes will go down easily with teachers unions and other groups that have traditionally controlled teacher certification. But for those concerned about the principle of local control, our proposal imposes few regulations from Washington. It aims instead to reduce regulation, for which there are no demonstrated benefits.

Transparency is already a major virtue of NCLB. Every school in America now receives a report card that enables families, citizens, policymakers, and the media to evaluate schools based on what should matter most—achievement of high academic standards. If schools fail to make progress, NCLB requires notice of that as well. If a student has a teacher who is not highly qualified, families are so informed. All the above information cannot help but improve schools. For too long, objective and consistent information about school performance was difficult to come by. Testing practices differed from district to district. Families knew the standardized test scores of their own children but nothing about the scores of their school or other schools. Most districts used national norm-referenced tests whose scores tended to drift upward over time, eventually exceeding national averages set many years earlier. As in the Garrison Keilor fantasy town of Lake Woebegon, all of the children appeared to be above average.

Now families and everyone else concerned with schools know better. Transparency should energize parents to become more involved with their schools. New information should increase the pressure on boards of education, superintendents, and state governments to make improvements. Yet NCLB needs to take transparency a step further. NCLB aims to improve public education not only by working through the traditional system; it aims to change the system—by promoting choice and competition, by providing options to students and families that the system would not otherwise provide. Here is where we find transparency sorely lacking. Districts have dragged their feet in informing parents about the opportunities to choose schools or to receive tutoring, a clear instance where giving school districts local control over a national goal was a bad compromise. Districts are conflicted and should therefore not be assigned this responsibility; it should be given to an independent agency.

Finally, there is the principle of *choice*. Local districts have been slow to cooperate with the requirements of NCLB, not only failing to provide parents with information but impeding implementation in multiple ways, as we have shown. This is a grave threat to the law's potential because the options that the law offers are the greatest break from federal school improvement efforts of the past. If schools fail students, students can get direct and immediate relief and do not need to wait for their school to improve, which heretofore had been the only option. But districts are not the right authorities to make the choice provisions of NCLB work because they have inherent conflicts of interest. Even working in good faith, districts will fall short, which is why we propose that choice and SES be overseen by independent agencies in each state. This proposal does not tread on state prerogatives because choice and SES are not services that public education has traditionally provided, but are new national initiatives that warrant independent administration.

We began our analysis of NCLB by noting that there have been many calls for midcourse corrections of this ambitious law—to make it fairer, more flexible, or more affordable. We conclude by reiterating that these recommendations largely miss the mark. The U.S. Department of Education has already been responsive to demands for fairness and flexibility. The rules for testing special education and limited English students have been relaxed. Requirements for teachers of multiple subjects in rural areas to be highly qualified have been delayed. Schools have been permitted to count the progress of students below proficiency toward AYP and to look at rolling averages of scores instead of annual results. The list goes on.[16] Meanwhile, the demands for more money are just more of the same. The direct costs of NCLB are fully funded, as the Government Accounting Office concluded in May 2004.[17] Indeed, from fiscal year 2000 through fiscal year 2004, appropriations for Title I grew by 56 percent and ESEA as a whole by 63 percent, well beyond any estimate of the direct cost of implementing the law's requirements.[18] The only thing not funded in NCLB is the cost of helping every child succeed—which is both incalculable and, in any case, the fundamental responsibility of public education. If there is to be a debate about money, it should not be about NCLB, it should be about the cost of public education generally.

Which brings us to the final cost: the cost of doing nothing. As Eric Hanushek reports in his chapter, the nation pays a high price for underachievement. Students with poor test scores do not finish high school and do not earn what it takes to survive. Students with mediocre test scores do not finish college and struggle to get by. If students raise their high school test scores by one standard deviation—considerably less than NCLB is aiming for—they can count on an additional $12,000 a year in earnings annually. If all students increased their scores by this amount, the nation's gross domestic product would increase by a full percentage point, a huge amount—enough to cover all of the costs of K-12 education today.

Achievement matters—and NCLB has unprecedented potential to improve it. As the law now stands, however, it will fall far short of that potential. NCLB has its goals and first principles absolutely right. But it has struck a bargain with local control that will prevent the law from truly working. To save NCLB—and it most certainly deserves saving—the law should be revised to strengthen its first principles. Accountability, transparency, and choice—the key drivers of NCLB—can be bolstered with practical reforms. Vital state and local prerogatives can be protected. America's public schools can be transformed.

Notes

1. Based on data for the 2003–2004 school year from twenty-nine states reporting from September 1, 2004, 13.8 percent of schools nationwide have "needs improvement" status and 30.4 percent failed to make AYP. Calculated from data in Lynn Olson, "Data Show Schools Making Progress on Federal Goals, *Education Week* 24, no. 2 (September 8, 2004): 1, 24–28.

2. Prominent examples include National Education Association, "Proposed Technical Amendments to NCLB" at www.nea.org (accessed April 7, 2003); Civil Rights Project at Harvard University, "Inspiring Vision, Disappointing Results: Four Studies on Implementing the No Child Left Behind Act" at www.civilrightsproject.harvard.edu (accessed February 2004); W. James Popham, "Shaping Up the 'No Child' Act," *Education Week* 23, no. 33 (May 26, 2004): 40; Linda Jacobsen and Beth Keller, "Union Delegates Give New Leader Go-Ahead to Attack Federal Law," *Education Week* 23, no. 42 (July 28, 2004): 9; and papers presented at the Center on Education Policy forum in Washington, D.C., in July 2004, as reported in Lynn Olson, "Critics Float 'No Child' Revisions," *Education Week* 23, no. 44 (August 11, 2004): 1, 33.

3. See chapter 2 by Diane Ravitch for elaboration.

4. See chapter 3 by Herbert Walberg for more detailed evidence and explanation.

5. Calculated from data in Lynn Olson, "Data Show Schools Making Progress on Federal Goals," *Education Week* 24, no. 2 (September 8, 2004): 1, 24–28.

6. For technical details, see chapter 4 by Caroline Hoxby.

7. In 2003, 77 percent of fourth graders were basic or above in math, and 63 percent were basic or above in reading; 32 percent were proficient or above in math and 31 percent were proficient or above in reading. In eighth grade the percentages were 68 percent and 63 percent basic or above in math and reading, respectively, and 29 percent and 31 percent proficient or above in math and reading, respectively. U.S. Department of Education, *NAEP: The Nation's Report Card*.

8. For details of the analysis, see chapter 5 by Eric Hanushek.

9. See chapter 6 by Williamson Evers and Lance Izumi for the complete story.

10. The sample includes the fifty U.S. districts with the greatest enrollment in 2000–2001, omitting districts that did not use the same tests in both 2001–2002 and 2002–2003.

11. Council of Great City Schools, *Beating the Odds IV* (Washington, D.C., March 2004).

12. For the specific methodology see chapter 4 by Caroline Hoxby.

13. Cited in Marilyn Marks, "Q and A: The Teacher Factor," *New York Times*, January 9, 2000, summarizing the findings of William Sanders and his renowned Tennessee value-added studies.

14. For the research supporting these claims and our full analysis of NCLB's teacher quality provisions, see chapter 7 by Terry Moe.

15. The research and findings reported in this section summarize the in-depth analysis provided by Paul Peterson in chapter 8.

16. See Eric Robelin, "States Gain More Leeway on Test Rule," *Education Week* 23, no. 30 (April 7, 2004).

17. David J. Hoff, "GAO: 'No Child' Law Is Not an 'Un-Funded Mandate,'" *Education Week* 23, no. 35 (June 9, 2004). Also see Peyser and Custrell, *Education Next*.

18. Based on actual appropriations, as reported by the U.S. Department of Education.

2

A Historical Perspective on a Historic Piece of Legislation

Diane Ravitch

Both supporters and critics of the No Child Left Behind (NCLB) legislation like to portray it as an initiative designed and pushed through Congress by President George W. Bush and modeled beforehand on his education reforms in Texas. The supporters do so because they want to credit President Bush with the first major domestic policy accomplishment of his administration. Critics attribute the law's centerpiece strategy of standards and accountability entirely to Bush so as to discredit it as partisan while attacking him and belittling the educational gains made in Texas during his governorship.

But those who attempt to portray NCLB as a purely Republican program based entirely on the Texas experience are wrong. Although President Bush surely deserves recognition for forging a strong bipartisan majority on behalf of a sweeping and historic overhaul of the federal role in education, the NCLB act did not spring full blown from his head nor was it uniquely Texan in origin. On the contrary, legislators and executives in both parties, in Washington and in the states, had advocated major elements of the new law during the previous two decades. Consequently, a federal strategy to improve education by focusing on results is likely to survive far into the future, regardless of which party controls the White House or Congress.

For most of American history, the federal government played an insignificant role in education. The word education does not appear in the Constitution; the governance and financing of schools have generally been viewed as state and local responsibilities. Advocates of federal aid to education aimed to equalize regional disparities in funding, but they usually failed to win congressional support because of disagreements about race, religion, and fears of an all-powerful federal bureaucracy. Some programs with specific goals did get enacted, such as aid for vocational education in 1917 and certain New Deal programs (including the Civilian Conservation Corps and the National Youth Administration). A major push for general federal aid to schools after World War II did not succeed, but a widespread fear of falling behind the Soviets in the space race produced the National Defense Education Act in 1958, which financed math, science, and foreign-language programs as well as new school construction.

The big breakthrough in federal financial support for schools occurred in 1965, when an overwhelmingly Democratic Congress passed President Lyndon B. Johnson's Elementary and Secondary Education Act (ESEA). Like every previous proposal for federal aid, ESEA was a response to a crisis, in this instance one provoked by the slow pace of desegregation, the demands of the civil rights movement, and violent riots in urban ghettos. ESEA pumped new money into urban schools with the goal of providing equality of educational opportunity for millions of poor children.

The vast majority of ESEA funding was allocated to Title I, which subsidized compensatory education programs and was distributed on a formula basis to almost every school district in the nation. The expectation of the program's sponsors was that the new, federally funded compensatory programs would raise the educational achievement of poor children. But some members of Congress were concerned that schools might use the federal funds to underwrite ineffective programs. A concerned senator Robert F. Kennedy of New York insisted that the law require school districts receiving Title I money to submit objective evaluations, at least annually, of the educational effectiveness of their programs. Senator Kennedy's concerns were soon realized, in that there was no single or comparable measure by which district-level Title I–funded programs could be judged. Many school districts never submitted the achievement data required by the law to the U.S. Office of Education. Even when districts submitted scores, the tests were so varied that the results were noncomparable to the point of being meaningless. Districts used Title I funding for a broad variety of programs, including remedial instruction, socialization skills, parent training, libraries, cultural enrichment, speech therapy, and medical services, meaning that the strategies, goals, and programs adopted by districts were so diffuse that it was not possible to meet the requirements of the law, compare districts across the country, or judge the efficacy of different approaches or programs.[1]

Despite the lack of any sure measure of its effectiveness in improving student achievement, Title I became a popular, well-established, and, in time, deeply entrenched program. Although it lacked evidence of student gains, it had all the earmarks of success: it was widely dispersed, it subsidized many state and local employees, and it symbolized the federal government's commitment to equality of educational opportunity. Every member of Congress had schools in his or her district receiving Title I funds, and everyone wanted to keep the money flowing to programs and activities for poor children. For a number of years, that goal—distributing the money—was seen as sufficient to the purpose of the legislation.

In 1975, however, a new educational issue captured public attention. Journalists noted that the SAT scores of college-bound students had fallen during the previous decade. Although the students who took those exams were not, in the main, the same students who were the beneficiaries of Title I and ESEA, the public became worried that the declining SAT scores signaled something wrong with the quality of American education. The College Board appointed a national commission to probe the reasons for the score decline, and President Jimmy Carter created study groups to examine weaknesses in mathematics, science, and foreign-language instruction. SAT scores continued to decline during the 1970s, and policymakers debated what was going wrong and what to do about it.

In 1980, Ronald Reagan was elected president. In his campaign, he pledged to abolish the Department of Education, which had been created in the closing months of the Carter administration. His choice for Secretary of Education, however, was Terrell Bell, a career educator who was deeply committed to enlarging the federal role in education, not eliminating it. Bell appointed the National Commission on Excellence in Education in August 1981 to examine the state of American education. The commission's 1983 report, *A Nation at Risk*, changed the education landscape. It acknowledged serious problems of underachievement, warned that the nation was undermining its future by tolerating educational mediocrity, and offered up a menu of reforms, including stronger graduation requirements, a more substantive curriculum, higher standards, more time for instruction, better teacher training, and more pay for teachers. By making education an important national issue, the report also made it impossible for Reagan to kill off the Department of Education.

The Excellence Commission report drew a clear connection between excellence and equity, anchoring its recommendations in the nation's historic commitment to equality of educational opportunity. Equity and high-quality schooling, said the commission, were conjoined twin goals, inextricably linked by the nature and ideals of our society. "Part of what is at risk," said the report, "is the promise first made on this continent: All, regardless of race or class or economic status, are entitled to a fair chance and to the tools for developing their individual powers of mind and spirit to the utmost. This promise means that all children by virtue of their own efforts, competently guided, can hope to attain the mature and informed judgment needed to secure gainful employment, and to manage their own lives, thereby serving not only their own interests but also the progress of society itself."[2]

After *A Nation at Risk* came a barrage of parallel reports, study groups, books, task forces, and commissions sponsored by private groups, individuals, foundations, states, and the federal government. Although a group appointed by President Reagan's secretary of education prepared the original *Nation at Risk* report, the response to it was entirely nonpartisan. The commission report had made a convincing, eloquent, and urgent case for educational improvement. Its analysis did not directly threaten any of education's major interest groups. Some critics in the academic world vigorously protested its findings about low achievement, but the report was generally met with appropriate alarm. Educators, professional associations, parent groups, civic groups, elected officials, legislatures, and all sorts of other concerned citizens took seriously the challenge described by the National Commission on Excellence in Education.

Southern governors became early champions of education reform. They recognized that their states' economic and social development was retarded by poor education. Prominent among the education-minded southern governors were Lamar Alexander (R.-Tennessee), Bill Clinton (D.-Arkansas), James B. Hunt (D.-North Carolina), and Richard Riley (D.-South Carolina). All agreed that the public schools in their states needed higher expectations, higher standards, and higher teachers' salaries; in a 1986 report called *Time for Results*, the National Governors Association (NGA) pledged to regulate schools less in exchange for an emphasis on improved academic achievement. The southern governors became leading activists within the NGA, where they pushed their campaign for education reform. Southern governors and the Southern Regional Education Board sought a common measure of student achievement so they could benchmark their students' progress and compare it to those represented in national and regional data. Consequently, in 1986, eight southern states administered the tests of the National Assessment of Education Progress to representative samples of their students.

Another by-product of the bipartisan focus on educational achievement was the creation of the National Assessment Governing Board (NAGB) in 1988 to oversee the National Assessment of Educational Progress (NAEP). This step was recommended a year previously by a commission chaired by Governor Lamar Alexander and H. Thomas James of the Spencer Foundation (among its members—named by Secretary of Education William Bennett—was Hillary Clinton, first lady of Arkansas).

The NAEP had been surveying student achievement since 1970 but big changes were now being made to it. The NAGB, the new independent oversight board for the national assessment, first agreed to devise standards, or achievement levels, so that student performance would be reported in relation to what students *should* know and be able to do; second, it sought and received congressional authorization to report on student performance not just for the nation but state by state. Both those decisions produced important new information about how American students were faring in such subjects as reading, mathematics, science, history, geography, civics, and the arts. The congressional authorization of changes in the national assessment was a product of bipartisan agreement, involving the Reagan Department of Education and Senator Edward Kennedy.

In 1989, responding to the growing interest in school reform, President George H.W. Bush convened the first-ever summit of the nation's governors. At their meeting in Charlottesville, Virginia, the president and governors reached agreement on the importance of setting national education goals. After much discussion between the White House and the National Governors Association (whose lead player was Governor Bill Clinton), President Bush announced six such goals for the year 2000 in his State of the Union address in 1990. The first goal said that all children would start school "ready to learn"; the second pledged that the high school graduation rate would rise to "at least 90 percent"; the third said that students would leave grades four, eight, and twelve "having demonstrated competency in challenging subject matter," including five subjects (English, mathematics, science, history, and geography); the fourth goal was that American students would lead the world in mathematics and science; the fifth goal promised that all American adults would be literate and prepared for work and citizenship; and the sixth pledged that "every school in America" would be safe and free of drugs. The National Education Goals Panel, which was established to monitor progress toward the goals, consisted of governors, members of Congress, representatives of the administration, and state legislators.

As soon as the new Goals Panel began its work, questions arose about how to measure progress toward the goals. It would not be difficult to measure the high school graduation rate or even adult literacy. But what did it mean to be "ready to learn"? How could that be measured? What was the meaning of "competency" and "challenging subject matter"? How could such questions be answered unless there were national standards and national tests? Yet how would such standards be set? Who would set them? Should they be voluntary or mandatory? What tests should be used to assess progress? What should be the role of the federal government?

To help answer these momentous questions, Congress established a thirty-two-member body called the National Council on Educational Standards and Testing. Cochaired by Governor Carroll A. Campbell Jr. (R.-South Carolina) and Governor Roy Romer (D.-Colorado), the council included leading members of both major political parties, as well as academics, educators, business leaders, and the presidents of the two largest teachers' unions. The council endorsed national standards and a "system of assessments" (not a single national test) and it proposed the creation of a new federal agency to work in conjunction with the National Education Goals Panel to "certify" standards and assessment. This agency, to be called the National Education Standards and Assessments Council, would be appointed by the National Education Goals Panel. The purpose of this arrangement was to remove national standards and assessments from partisan politics.

In 1991, President George H. W. Bush launched his program of education reform, which he called America 2000. Among other things, the America 2000 plan called for voluntary national testing tied to "world-class standards." The problem, however, was that no such standards existed, nor were there any prospects for establishing national testing, at least not by the federal government. The obstacles to the president's America 2000 plan were many: Republicans were a minority in both houses of Congress; some Republicans were opposed to a federally controlled national testing system; and Democrats were unwilling to give any legislative accomplishments to President Bush in an election year. Thus, there was no possibility of getting congressional authorization to create national testing or to enact any other part of the America 2000 agenda. As it happened, in 1988 Congress had authorized the Department of Education to develop a high school test of academic excellence, at the urging of Democratic senator Claiborne Pell; the Bush administration, however, did not try to utilize opening because it was clearly enacted for a different purpose.

On the standards front, the Department of Education, the National Endowment for the Humanities, and the National Science Foundation supported the development of voluntary national standards by professional subject matter associations. Undertaken in the last eighteen months of the administration's life, this activity was rushed and fatally flawed by a lack of administrative planning, supervisory oversight, and coordination among the groups. Each cluster of educators saw the invitation to develop a standards document as a wish list. None of the groups needed to consider classroom time constraints or to recognize that other subjects needed time in the school day. Each group of grant recipients eventually produced a document titled "Voluntary National Standards," but no process or agency existed to review, improve, reject, or approve them. A few, notably mathematics, gained traction within the profession, but others, notably English and history, were met with heavy criticism on their release.

The winner of the 1992 election, Bill Clinton, had been one of the most active of the education-minded southern governors; in Arkansas, he had pressed for higher standards and new tests for both students and teachers. The Clinton-Gore campaign document ("Putting People First") pledged that the new administration would "establish tough standards and a national examination system." President Clinton selected former governor Richard Riley as his secretary of education; Riley, as governor of South Carolina, had raised taxes to pay for higher standards. Because President Clinton had been a key figure in framing the national goals, his administration's education initiative was titled Goals 2000. It passed Congress in March 1994, adding two new goals to the previous six: one promising that all teachers would have access to professional development programs, and another pledging to increase parental participation in schooling. Goals 2000 encouraged all states to develop their own standards and assessments and provided funding for them to do so. The legislation also provided for a National Education Standards and Improvement Council (akin to the earlier proposal by the National Council on Educational Standards and Testing); its purpose would be to review and certify state and national standards and assessments, subject to the approval of the National Education Goals Panel. However, when control of Congress shifted to the Republicans in 1994, the standards council became a dead letter owing to Republican opposition. Although it was enacted into law, President Clinton and congressional leaders never nominated anyone to serve on the council. Nonetheless, Goals 2000 distributed federal funding to almost every state to develop curriculum frameworks (i.e., statements of what students are expected to learn in each subject) and new tests aligned with the frameworks.

The reauthorization of the Elementary and Secondary Education Act in 1994 reinforced the need for every state to adopt standards and tests and to make sure that children benefiting from Title I funds were prepared to meet the new standards. The 1994 legislation contained new accountability provisions, but many states failed to comply, largely because the sanctions against such states were weak.

During his eight years in office, President Clinton was an eloquent advocate for higher standards and national testing. In his 1997 State of the Union message, he called for the creation of voluntary national testing of reading in fourth grade and mathematics in eighth grade. Clinton knew there was overwhelming public support for standards and tests. He believed that parents and educators needed information about student performance based on common measures. After the Department of Education awarded a contract to a consortium of testing agencies, the management and development of the new tests was turned over to the National Assessment Governing Board to ensure that the tests were as rigorous as those of the NAEP. However, the voluntary national tests died because Congress never authorized them. The majority Republicans were unwilling to turn that much power over the nation's schools to the federal government, and many congressional democrats were unenthusiastic about testing.

In 1997, the National Education Goals Panel identified two states—North Carolina and Texas—as having made the greatest gains on thirty-three indicators linked to the national goals. That panel then commissioned David Grissmer of the Rand Corporation to analyze the factors that had contributed to the steady improvement in those states. The two states, Grissmer found, had followed similar paths. They had created an aligned system of standards, curriculum, and assessments; they had held schools accountable for improvement by all students; and they had rallied significant support from the business community in implementing their reforms. Both states' policies contained common elements that were key to their improvement:

First, the states adopted statewide standards, grade by grade so that teachers in each grade knew what their students were expected to learn.

Second, they held *all* students to the same standards. Disadvantaged students were held to the same standards as their advantaged peers. Only students with significant learning disabilities were exempted. In addition, Texas disaggregated student test results by race, ethnicity, and the socioeconomic status of the students. Schools had to meet performance targets for all these groups.

Third, both states adopted statewide testing aligned to their standards. Students in both states were tested annually from grades three through eight. North Carolina began its state testing in 1992–1993, Texas in 1993–1994.

Fourth, both states had accountability systems with consequences for results. Schools were rated for their students' test performance, with the primary ranking mechanism being academic gain scores, but absolute levels of performance were also considered. Those that improved won monetary awards. Those that did not were subject to a variety of sanctions, including the removal of principals.

Fifth, both states shifted more authority and flexibility to the school site. Regulations were reduced to encourage administrators and teachers to vary their approaches and focus on results.

Sixth, the states created computerized feedback systems so that data could promptly flow to parents, students, teachers, and schools and be used for continuous improvement.

Seventh, both states shifted additional funds to those schools with many disadvantaged students. Although the motive may have been compliance with judicial decisions, the effect was to enhance the perception of fairness in the system.[3]

The Grissmer study was widely discussed and read by policymakers in Washington and state capitals because it was sponsored by the National Education Goals Panel, which was known to be scrupulously nonpartisan and dominated by elected state officials from outside the Beltway. The panel consisted of eight governors, four state legislators, two representatives of the administration in power, and four members of Congress. Thus, Grissmer's study received attention among policymakers at the same time that the Clinton administration's Goals 2000 law was urging states to adopt similar strategies of standards, assessments, and accountability for school improvement.

In the run-up to the 2000 election, the political parties began jousting over educational strategies. Each contained a diversity of views about the best policy direction and the correct federal role in education. Among Republicans, there were proponents of block grants, vouchers, and a sharply diminished federal role, as well as proponents of the Texas/North Carolina strategy of standards, assessments, and accountability. Among Democrats, there were proponents of what might be called the status quo, that is, more spending, more regulation, and little or no accountability for results; but there were also Democrats who believed strongly in the strategy of standards, assessments, and accountability for results, as well as public school choice. Among Republicans, Governor George W. Bush was the most outspoken leader of the standards strategy, which he believed would benefit all children but especially those whose failure was hidden in statistical averages. As a candidate for the presidency, Bush spoke often about his plan to improve education and about the importance of rejecting what he called "the soft bigotry of low expectations." The Democratic candidate, Vice President Albert Gore, also was a strong supporter of standards and accountability, which was a continuation of the Clinton administration's approach to education.

The election year discussion was influenced in large part by two think tanks in Washington, D.C. One, the Thomas B. Fordham Foundation, was led by Chester E. Finn Jr., who had been an assistant secretary in the Reagan administration. The other, the Progressive Policy Institute, was known for its close association with the Clinton-Gore administration; its spokesman was Andrew Rotherham, who had served as President Clinton's education adviser. Finn and Rotherham (and their respective organizations) sponsored a joint conference on the future reauthorization of ESEA in December 1998, drawing speakers from across the political spectrum. What was remarkable was the extent of agreement between their respective views about the federal role in education.

In March 1999, the Fordham Foundation published a series of essays about the failure of Title I to improve the academic achievement of poor children. Looking ahead to the upcoming reauthorization of the Elementary and Secondary Act, Finn, writing with his colleagues Marci Kanstoroom and Michael Petrilli, pointed out that the federal government had spent more than $100 billion on Title I over three decades with no demonstrable academic gains for the disadvantaged students who were its intended beneficiaries. They wrote that ESEA had become a grab bag of miscellaneous programs, with little or no credible claims to success, and identified three overriding priorities for the next round of federal lawmaking.

First, they argued that federal policymakers should show "restraint—and political courage—by committing to academic achievement to the exclusion of all else. . . . There is one and only one transcendent national education objective worthy of being enshrined in federal policy in 1999: higher academic achievement for all students and schools." Washington, said Finn and his colleagues, should "make sure all of its programs aim toward that end, and eliminate all incentives and practices that distract or confuse schools in their pursuit of that end."

Second, Finn asked, who should be entrusted with money and control to ensure that our national priorities are met? In the past, money and control were vested in federal bureaucrats and local school districts. Finn recommended instead that the main actors in school reform should be states and parents. The states, he wrote, had the "primary constitutional authority" for schooling and had demonstrated a zeal for reform and experimentation that far exceeded anything seen at the local level. Parents, he maintained, had traditionally been excluded from decisions about the fate of their children, but they were best qualified to make "wise educational decisions" on their behalf. He urged the removal of barriers to parental choice, especially the parents of disadvantaged children—the very children that Title I was supposed to serve—who were so frequently trapped in unacceptable schools.

Third, Finn urged a fundamental shift from a compliance-driven system to one based on "academic performance and customer satisfaction." Traditionally, states and school districts met federal requirements if they were able to demonstrate that they had "followed all the rules and procedures and spent all their federal dollars on approved activities" for specified groups of students. His advice: Give states and communities more flexibility but hold them accountable for "demonstrable results," meaning improved academic performance.[4]

Andrew Rotherham's analyses of the changes needed in ESEA appeared in April 1999 and were closely aligned with those of the Gore campaign. Rotherham called for a thorough overhaul of ESEA, converting it from a $13 billion crazy quilt of more than fifty programs into a performance-based system that would leverage large-scale improvements in public education across the nation. ESEA, he wrote, "is best viewed as a welter of spending dictates that prescribe how states and localities must spend federal dollars but does not hold them accountable for achieving measurable improvements." He urged support for a "new bargain. . . . States and localities should get increased flexibility for using federal resources but must take increased responsibility for results." ESEA, he wrote, had mushroomed over the years into "a confusing, unfocused, and largely ineffective statute, as a result of interest group pressure, constituency politics, and Washington's inability to eliminate or consolidate even the smallest or least effective government program."

What was needed, Rotherham urged, was to stop using federal education dollars as a guaranteed source of revenue and to turn them instead into leverage for higher student performance. This would occur only if Congress insisted on true accountability for performance, with actual benchmarks for states and localities, and palpable consequences for states and districts that consistently failed to meet established benchmarks. The overall goal of the coming reauthorization, Rotherham hoped, would be to replace categorical programs with fewer, larger, and more flexible performance-based grants.[5]

The campaigns of both Bush and Gore supported education reforms that would promote results rather than compliance. Bush relied on his experience as governor of Texas, and Gore relied on his experience as vice president. Both argued for standards and accountability.

Soon after the inauguration of President George W. Bush in January 2001, his administration immediately set to work to gain passage of his signature education program, called No Child Left Behind. This program had been a major focus of his campaign and a major activity of his postelection transition. NCLB built on the familiar strategy of standards, assessments, and accountability that had emerged from nearly two decades of bipartisan cooperation. It incorporated principles that had been raised by *A Nation at Risk*, the national goals process, America 2000, Goals 2000, and the reauthorization of ESEA in 1994. In the course of negotiating the bill, there were many compromises and changes. Many features were added that did not exist in the Texas education reform program, such as adequate yearly progress with a certain date for reaching a target of 100 percent proficiency. The administration was eager to win passage of the legislation and to stand up alongside the leaders of both parties, so the final bill represented a broad consensus that satisfied many constituencies. On final passage of the Senate-House conference report, the No Child Left Behind bill was endorsed in the House by a vote of 381-41 and in the Senate by a vote of 87-10. President Bush proudly acknowledged the important roles played by Senator Edward Kennedy (D.-Mass.), Senator Judd

Gregg (R.-Kansas), Congressman George Miller (D.-Calif.), and Congressman John Boehner (D.-Ohio) in shaping the bill. He even took the extraordinary step of signing the bill at multiple sites around the country, including the districts or states of its major congressional sponsors, where leaders of both parties shared credit for the most important overhaul of federal education policy since 1965.

As with the 1994 reauthorization of ESEA, NCLB required states to set standards, conduct assessments, and use the information derived from the assessments to hold schools accountable for student performance. Unlike the 1994 reauthorization, however, NCLB required states to disaggregate the academic achievement of students by their race, gender, ethnicity, special education status, and whether they were limited English proficient. In the past, the academic progress of some of these categories had been obscured in overall averages. The point of No Child Left Behind was to make sure that schools were held accountable for the progress of *every* child. In the past, a school district might win plaudits for its achievements even though racial minority students were lagging far behind; under NCLB, the performance of subgroups could no longer be hidden or overlooked. Two prominent civil rights lawyers, James S. Liebman and Charles F. Sabell, argued in law review articles in 2003 that NCLB was the "legitimate legatee" of the civil rights movement because it inspired mechanisms and structural changes in the delivery of education services that benefit low-income students.[6]

There is no doubt that NCLB is historic legislation. It has changed the nature of the federal role. The U.S. Department of Education was previously an agency that wrote checks; now one of its most important roles is to monitor continuous academic improvement from states, districts, and schools. Now states must test every child from grades three through eight in reading and mathematics (and eventually in science) to demonstrate whether they are making academic gains. (Although NCLB is theoretically voluntary, it does apply to all states that accept Title I money, which all states do.) NCLB has focused attention on achievement gaps among children from different groups by forcing the data about these gaps into the open. Because the law demands that subgroups improve their performance, schools and school districts have been scrambling to find better strategies to help disadvantaged youngsters and discouraged learners. Like the 1994 reauthorization of ESEA, NCLB sidestepped the thorny issue of national standards and national testing by requiring the states to use their own; state reporting on student gains is checked, however, by state performance on the NAEP. States now must participate in regular NAEP assessments of reading and mathematics to show that their claims of academic progress ring true.

NCLB is the culmination of a long, steady process that was constructed and abetted by Democrats and Republicans alike. Some in each party opposed the standards and accountability strategy—Republicans because of their objection to an enlarged federal role and their enthusiasm for school choice, Democrats because of their preference for more spending with minimal conditions—but the mainstream in both parties decisively embraced this approach. History demonstrates that it is possible to have a federal education strategy that consists of distributing money without demanding results, just as it is possible to have no federal role in education at all. But in the early years of the twenty-first century, those strategies appear to be obsolete. The public does not want to see the federal role in education eliminated. National polls consistently reveal overwhelming public support for standards and testing.

Teachers, sports teams, and business leaders have long known that measuring performance matters. Incentives matter. The absence of incentives also matters. These ideas would be considered axiomatic in any other profession or line of endeavor. This is why the principles embedded in NCLB are not likely to go away. In years to come, the law may be improved, and its provisions and regulations may be adjusted, but its underlying assumptions are rooted in a longstanding desire by both parties to measure the academic progress made by students. For this reason, it is likely to survive, no matter which party controls Congress or the White House in the future.

Notes

1. Diane Ravitch, *The Troubled Crusade: American Education, 1945–1980* (New York: Basic Books), 160.

2. National Commission on Excellence in Education, *A Nation at Risk* (Washington, D.C.: U.S. Government Printing Office, 1983), 8, 13.

3. David Grissmer and Ann Flanagan, "Exploring Rapid Achievement Gains in North Carolina and Texas," National Education Goals Panel, Washington, D.C., November 1998.

4. Chester E. Finn Jr., Marci Kanstoroom, and Michael J. Petrilli, "Overview: Thirty-four Years of Dashed Hopes," in *New Directions: Federal Education Policy in the Twenty-first Century* (Washington, D.C.: Thomas B. Fordham Foundation, March 1999), 1–16.

5. Andrew Rotherham, "Toward Performance-Based Federal Education Funding: Reauthorization of the ESEA," Progressive Policy Institute, April 1, 1999.

6. James S. Liebman and Charles F. Sabel, "A Public Laboratory Dewey Barely Imagined: The Emerging Model of School Governance and Legal Reform," *N.Y.U. J. L. & Soc. Change* 28 (2002–2003); see also James S. Liebman, "The Federal No Child Left Behind Act and the Post-Desegregation Civil Rights Agenda," *No. Car. L. Rev.* 81, no. 1703 (2003).

3

Standards, Testing, and Accountability

Herbert J. Walberg

The federal No Child Left Behind Act sustains and magnifies the federal role in education begun with the passage of the Elementary and Secondary Education Act of 1965 and continued through the Improving America's Schools Act of 1994 and Goals 2000 Act. This chapter describes the standards, testing, and accountability challenges of NCLB. It portrays the states' complying with the act's requirements and suggests improvements in federal and state policies. Before turning to the specific requirements of NCLB, it may be useful to review evidence that the testing and accountability it calls for not only raise achievement but also may be some of the most cost-efficient policies available to legislators and educators.

Effects and Costs of Accountability

What is the direct evidence of beneficial accountability effects? A 2001 Education Trust study found 4,500 schools in forty-seven states that served more than a million high-poverty and more than a million minority students and that performed among the top one-third of schools in their states. These schools often outperformed predominantly white schools in advantaged communities.[1]

The common features of these exceptionally performing schools included (1) the use of state standards to design curriculum and instruction, ongoing assessment of student work, and teacher evaluation, (2) comprehensive systems to monitor individual student progress and provide extra support to students as soon as needed, and (3) state accountability systems that have real consequences for professionals in the schools. A similar study of successful school districts showed that they (1) nurtured high expectations and focused on achievement results, (2) aligned curricula and instruction to state standards and tests, and (3) provided frequent testing, practice, and reteaching for students in need of help.[2]

A recent analysis showed state achievement gains on the National Assessment of Educational Progress (NAEP) were related to the quality of their systems. Texas, North Carolina, New Jersey, and Florida were rated highest because they had extensive testing, school report cards, high school exit examinations, and consequences for school staff. High levels of accountability led to higher NAEP score gains, particularly those of African American and Hispanic students.[3] Contrary to prevalent hand-wringing, stronger accountability did not reduce promotion or increase dropout rates but raised measures of both lower-order and higher-order learning. Surprisingly, the study showed that strong accountability reduced teacher turnover, which suggests goal-directed, results-oriented schools are not only more productive but more pleasant than schools where whims reign. Accountability for meeting common standards not only provides information for rational decision making but also increases the likelihood that students, particularly at-risk students, will not miss crucial knowledge and skills they need for subsequent learning and, we can hope, for life beyond school.

Test costs are surprisingly small and represent a tiny percentage of K–12 budgets. For twenty-five states with available information, accountability costs of about $20 per student were only about 0.3 percent of the average costs of around $7,250 per student. Such costs, moreover, may decline in the longer run since they were estimated in the midst of states' development of accountability systems. After development and initial revision, much of the activity can be routinized to reduce costs and afford broader accountability.[4] With more time and experience, both lower costs and greater achievement improvement can be expected. It seems reasonable to think that all or nearly all students can make substantial gains in proficiency by the year 2014 as NCLB projects.

NCLB Test and Accountability Requirements

By instituting testing and accountability as centerpieces of the education agenda, President George W. Bush and Congress reinforced central themes of state policies aimed at improving education through testing and accountability. The purpose of the NCLB Act is to ensure that all children have the opportunity to obtain a high-quality education and reach, at a minimum, proficiency on state academic achievement standards as revealed by state assessments.

The states are responsible for developing content and performance standards and assessments. The legislation, nonetheless, increases the federal oversight of the size, scope, and nature of the states' accountability systems. The states, for example, are required in principle to adhere to the requirements in chart 1.

NCLB Accountability Principles

The U.S. Department of Education (DOE) developed a Consolidated Application Accountability Workbook[5] that extended each of the NCLB accountability principles into more specific critical elements with examples. States then had a common framework and were required to submit their completed workbooks outlining their accountability plans by January 31, 2003. The states had to provide evidence on the ten principles in chart 2. These seem reasonable principles that merit adherence, support, and continuation.

Chart 3.1 NCLB Standards-Related Requirements

- Adopt challenging academic content standards and develop new state tests that are aligned with the standards.
- Develop valid and reliable testing programs for grades 3–8 in reading and mathematics and in one high school grade. These tests are to be implemented by the 2005–2006 school year.
- Apply the same alignment between science content standards and a state science test to be administered at least one time during grades 3–5, 6–9, and 10–12, beginning in the 2007–2008 school year.
- Develop challenging student academic achievement standards with a minimum of three performance levels—advanced, proficient, and basic.
- Produce individual student interpretive, descriptive, and diagnostic reports that allow parents, teachers, and principals to understand and address the specific academic needs of students.
- Apply the same content and achievement standards to all schools and school age children in the state; that is, expect the same knowledge, skills, and level of achievement of all students.
- Include separate and measurable annual achievement objectives for continuous and substantial improvement for the following special subgroups of students: economically disadvantaged, students from major racial and ethnic groups, students with disabilities, and students with limited English proficiency. The objectives must adhere to the goal that all students attain the proficient level or above within twelve years (i.e., by the end of the 2013–2014 school year.)
- Establish procedures for schools requiring at least 95 percent of all its students (including 95 percent of the students in each of the above subgroups) to participate annually in the state's assessment.
- Develop indicators of progress other than academic achievement; such indicators may include attendance at elementary schools and graduation rates at high school.

Chart 3.2 NAEP Accountability Principles

- A single statewide accountability system is applied to all public schools and local education authorities (LEAs), usually school districts.
- All students are included in the state accountability system.
- The state definition of adequate yearly progress (AYP) is based on expectations for growth in student achievement that is continuous and substantial, so that all students are proficient in reading/language arts and mathematics no later than 2013–2014.
- The states make annual decisions about the achievement of all public schools and LEAs.
- All public schools and LEAs are held accountable for the achievement of individual groups.
- The state definition of AYP is based primarily on the state's academic assessments.
- The state definition of AYP includes a graduation rate for public high schools and an additional indicator selected by the state for public middle and elementary schools (such as attendance rates).
- AYP is based on reading/language arts and mathematics achievement objectives.
- The state accountability system is statistically valid and reliable.
- In order for a public school or LEA to make AYP, the state ensures that it assesses at least 95 percent of the students enrolled in each subgroup.

Will NCLB Work?

Will the ambitious plans actually be implemented according to schedule? History may provoke doubt. A report from the Council of Chief State School Officers observed that "by January 2002, when NCLB took effect, only about one-third of the states had fully met the standards and assessment requirements for NCLB's predecessor, the Improving America's Schools Act of 1994."[6] Many states were still working toward completion of academic content standards and student performance standards, along with assessments aligned with these standards.

In addition, the Chiefs' report notes that, despite the NCLB legislation and review, the states interpreted the NCLB requirements in various ways.[7] Because the state accountability systems varied considerably in complexity and quality, the states differed in their capacity to help local districts engage in school improvement. These variations meant it was difficult to compare the progress of the states in implementing the act and estimate its effects on achievement.

However, recent analyses of state accountability show substantial improvements after NCLB. The twenty-nine states (and the District of Columbia) that were available for analysis clustered around a rating of "fair" before NCLB but were rated near "solid" afterward.[8]

The Education Commission of the States corroborates this good news about progress in testing and accountability.[9] In 2004, forty-eight states had met or were partially on track to meeting 75 percent of the law's requirements, a doubling over 2003. Standards and assessment adherence, moreover, was generally higher than with other areas, such as teacher quality (see Table 3.1).

Table 3.1.   No Child Left Behind Standards

	Number of States Meeting Standards
Standards and Assessments	
Reading standards established	40
Mathematics standards established	38
Annual assessment in reading & language arts	30
Annual assessment in mathematics	29
Report cards	19
Teacher Quality	
Test for new elementary teachers	43
Highly qualified teacher definition	23
Subject matter competence	11
Highly qualified teacher in every classroom	0
High-quality professional development	0

Unlike many previous federal K–12 education initiatives, these are signs of substantial progress. As Chester Finn noted, "We didn't fully fathom the arduousness of moving from broad goals to specific, high-quality content standards, demanding performance standards, workable assessments and forceful high-stakes accountability systems."[10] He finds, however, that where states have all of these elements in place, educators can see them paying off to a degree that justifies the effort. As discussed above, evidence-based analyses support his view.[11] In addition, the surveys discussed above reveal that further progress is being made. Thus, contrary to the usual reservations of all professions about accountability, the measurement–carrot-and-stick approach appears to be working.

Content, Standards, and Accountability

NCLB continues on course with standards-based reform and encourages states to adopt ambitious subject matter standards. Although the requirements for the standards and assessments under NCLB are rigorous, they represent an expansion of the previous requirements, not a foray into entirely new territory. Educators have long recognized the importance of valid assessment:

> Because tests can affect what is taught so powerfully, policymakers need to ensure that state tests actually measure what they were intended to measure. Otherwise, educators will be chasing the wrong goal, and policymakers will not have a good gauge of whether schools are producing the desired results.[12]

In the standards tradition, the term "alignment" means that tests validly measure content standards. Such alignment is based on the commonsense assumption that means should reflect ends and that progress in achieving ends requires measurement. Student achievement should improve under such principles if the curriculum materials, staff development, instructional strategies, and classroom assessments are coordinated with one another instead of pulling in different directions.

If the content standards are too general and vague, it will be difficult to develop a valid test because the test constructors would have to guess at what was intended. Reliability is also likely to suffer because independent groups working from the same vague standards are likely to produce assessments that are poorly correlated with one another.[13]

Some test experts are concerned that high-stakes tests in state accountability systems might lead to a narrowed instructional focus on the test at the expense of other important material.[14] The solution to this possible problem is broader standards and valid assessments to measure them. If all the content cannot be tested, then sampling within areas of content can play an efficient role just as it does in citizen sampling in surveys.

On the possibly controversial matter of content standards, one prominent test authority points out that "almost every state has adopted content standards for the areas of reading/language arts and mathematics. They vary greatly in their specificity, and arguably, in their degree of difficulty, but each state will be able to claim that their content standards are in compliance with NCLB."[15]

NCLB, however, requires states to participate in the National Assessment of Educational Progress, a well-regarded set of valid and reliable examinations that yield reasonable estimates of proficiency levels. Corroborating the contention above, some states may have had relatively low standards in that far fewer of their students meet NAEP standards than met state standards.[16] Given the growing prominence of NCLB and NAEP test results, however, slack standards and performance should become readily apparent to state and national policymakers, educators, citizens, and parents. (I provide evidence on this point later in the chapter.)

The Thomas B. Fordham Foundation usefully defined and analyzed state standards and accountability, according to which good standards are rigorous, clear, written in plain English, communicate what is expected of students, and assessable. Good accountability systems are aligned with the standards and include report cards, school ratings, rewards for successful schools, authority to reconstitute failing schools (for example, by replacing the staff), and the exercise of such legislated consequences.

Only five states—Alabama, California, North Carolina, South Carolina, and Texas—have solid standards and strong accountability systems. The Fordham Report is a good starting point for assessing and improving standards and accountability. States can find their strengths and weaknesses and plan improvements. Several additional accountability and assessment principles deserve analysis here.

Norm-Referenced and Criterion-Referenced Tests

How will states determine that content standards have been achieved? Historically, many state education agencies and local districts have chosen a norm-referenced test from a publisher that provides comparative information on student performance against other students. For example, a student in Chicago receives a score on the Iowa Test of Basic Skills. That student's performance is then compared to students across the country using the extensive national normative studies conducted by the publisher. The student may receive a grade equivalent score, percentile rank, stanine, normal curve equivalent score, or all of the above. The percentile rank provides information on student performance relative to the "norm group," the result of administering the test to a national sample.

A percentile rank shows where the student performs relative to a national sample or other norm group. It gives no indication of the student's mastery of content standards. The content and skills assessed by norm-referenced tests (NRTs) may or may not be included in a particular state's content standards. Dozens of such traditional and reliable off-the-shelf, norm-referenced tests can be readily purchased for large-scale administration to compare students to other students. These tests, however, are not designed specifically to report whether state content standards have been attained. For this purpose, the best but most costly and time-consuming solution is to develop new criterion-referenced tests (CRTs) that align with the state's standards.

But test items are not inherently criterion- or norm-referenced. Consider the item "Given a fraction's denominator of 4 and an answer of 0.5, what is the numerator?" That question could be on either a norm- or a criterion-referenced test in that a student's or school's scores based on the item (and other mathematics items) could be reported relative to a national sample or to the proficiency scale in a state's standards.

A hybrid approach, particularly practical in the short term, employs parts or all of off-the-shelf commercial normative tests augmented by unique state items to generate both normative and proficiency scores. Thus, high levels of proficiency on low standards in a school, district, or state would be made clear by a quick comparison. As explained subsequently, comparison with NAEP scores provides another check on the rigor of a state's standards.

A hybrid approach in conjunction with the annual requirement for reading and mathematics tests in grades three through eight may be ideal. Then, in principle, the value-added influence of each grade, means of instruction, and even individual teacher on the students' learning could be assessed. How much can a norm-referenced test be modified or supplemented before it loses its validity to measure national norms and state proficiency levels? Questions such as this will provide the U.S. Department of Education, states, and experts with continuing sources of study and discussion.

Several states are phasing out NRTs in favor of new CRTs or shifting to hybrid or augmented NRTs.[17] States using NRTs for Annual Yearly Progress purposes are required to ensure that they are "augmented with additional items as necessary to measure accurately the depth and breadth of the state's academic standards." Former U.S secretary of education Rodney Paige declared that student results from an augmented, nationally normed assessment must be expressed in terms of the state's achievement standards—not relative to other students in the nation.[17] This declaration does not exclude NRT reporting; it would be advantageous, as mentioned above, for policymakers, educators, and parents to have both kinds of reporting.

Professional and Technical Standards

The NCLB Act states that assessments will be consistent with relevant, nationally recognized professional and technical standards. States must provide evidence from the test developer, publisher, or other relevant sources that the provided assessments are of adequate technical quality and that the evidence can be made public by the secretary on request.

Nationally recognized professional and technical standards include the *Standards for Educational and Psychological Testing* developed by the American Educational Research Association, the American Psychological Association, and the National Council on Measurement in Education.[18] Because the "test standards are widely recognized as the most authoritative statements of professional consensus regarding expectations for tests on matters of validity, fairness and other technical characteristics of tests," state authorities may wish to consider how their plans fit both the NCLB requirements and the professional test standards.[19]

The test standards, however, are not the only consideration. The writers of those standards are not the responsible parties for federal, state, and local policy and thus may not have considered the legislators' concern about raising achievement. They wrote before the evidence that showed that accountability has worked well in improving students' learning. They may not have considered the relative costs and benefits of testing policies and practices, and thus their views may not weigh most heavily in the minds of decision makers.

The perfect can be the enemy of the good, and the good delayed may be the good abandoned for another generation of students. Congress and state legislatures have chosen to move forward in an effort to improve achievement using tests that may have various minor to moderate but remediable shortcomings. The assessments should improve with time and experience. Or professional opinion may change in the light of recent evidence and be reflected in a new edition of the test standards. In any case, the test standards are worth considering, to suggest improvements.

Validity

In this chapter, test validity and reliability are primary considerations. According to the standards, "Validity refers to the degree to which evidence and theory support the interpretation of tests. The process of validation involves accumulating evidence to provide sound scientific basis for the proposed score interpretations."[20] Among the most important standards for NCLB, Standard 1.1 states that "a rationale should be presented for each recommended interpretation and use of test scores, together with a comprehensive summary of the evidence and theory bearing on the intended use or interpretation."[21]

Therefore, in developing assessments required by NCLB, "content validity" (or test alignment to the content standards) is critical because students' proficiency determines whether schools have met adequate yearly progress (AYP). Reviews of the items by expert judges (including teachers in the particular grade and field) can ensure that the items do measure the content standards. The adequacy of the set of items representing the content should be described in explicit detail.

Validity implies comprehensiveness. Assessments in only a few grades may be invalid in estimating the progress of the entire school, and such a narrow policy could encourage educators to assign the best teachers and the most resources to only the grade levels tested. The NCLB requirement that grades three through eight are tested by the 2005–2006 school year enlarges the comprehensiveness and validity of the accountability systems.

As called for by NCLB, the number of grades tested should be expanded, as well as the subjects and the statistical reporting, even beyond present NCLB requirements. For example, if only mathematics, reading, and science are tested, then writing, civics, and history may be neglected.

Similarly, if only proficiency is reported, schools may concentrate their efforts on the few students near the proficiency milestones, and neglect both those students who have already passed them and those with little hope of soon attaining them. One solution is to report, as does the National Assessment of

Educational Progress, the percentages of students below basic, basic, proficient, and advanced. Even conventional tests of reasonable length, however, cannot easily estimate all those percentages well.

Computer-adaptive testing potentially eliminates this problem because it customizes the selection of test items to the student and cuts the number of items administered to a given student by as much as 75 percent. The scores are immediately available, and such tests can be administered frequently at will as the occasion requires.

Another solution is to calculate and report average (arithmetic mean) scores in addition to proficiency percentages. Averages are based on all eligible students in the school or subgroup. Such averages give equal weight to each student, no matter what his or her score.[22]

Standard 1.7 explains the role of expert judges: "Systematic collection of judgments or opinions may occur at many points in test construction (e.g., in eliciting expert judgments of content appropriateness or adequate content representation), in formulating rules or standards for score interpretation (e.g., in setting cut scores), or in test scoring (e.g., rating of essay responses). Whenever such processes are employed, the quality of the resulting judgments is important in the validation."[23] For assessments in development, expert judgments are made by committees of subject matter experts and educators familiar with the content of the grade levels and subject areas. The committees review items for content coverage and set proficiency cut scores for grade levels.

If standards and assessments cover a limited domain of skill, then any inferences must be limited to that domain.[24] On occasion, specific and concrete standards may sometimes themselves best define the domain of knowledge and skills suggested by the standards. Some behavioral outcomes such as keyboarding, diving, and first aid may be expressed in detail, such as keyboarding thirty words a minute with five errors per thousand words. Most standards of course must be more broadly defined, and as suggested above, sampling may be employed. Sampling from large pools of items can help minimize "teaching the test." Writing a new set of test items each year, as in Texas, can also minimize teaching-the-test effects.

Because inferences beyond the domain of the test may be questionable, a blueprint should be developed to specify the scope and parts of the test and the number of test items for each part.[25] The blueprint can be useful not only in designing and evaluating the test but also in informing educators, parents, and the public about the nature and scope of the test. Two-way grids for item classification are useful in showing both content, such as the causes of the Civil War, and cognitive levels, such as factual knowledge, conceptual understanding, and critical thinking.

Reliability

According to the standards, "A test, broadly defined, is a set of tasks designed to describe examinee behavior in a specified domain, or a system for collecting samples of an individual's work in a particular area. Coupled with the device is a scoring procedure that enables the examiner to quantify, evaluate, and interpret behavior or work samples. Reliability refers to the consistency of such measurements when the testing procedure is repeated on a population of individuals or groups."[26] Test developers therefore should present evidence of reliability and error measurement.

Standard 2.1 states: "For each total score, subscore, or combination of scores that is to be interpreted, estimates of relevant reliabilities and standard errors of measurement or test information functions should be reported."[27] This standard is applicable not only to total scores for all students but also for each subgroup. Given that some of these subgroups will be small and that AYP will be based on their scores, test reliability across a large range of scores may be critical. Because test reliability is often a function of the number of items (other things being equal), longer tests are more reliable.

Colorado research indicates that school-level results are often volatile from year to year because of differences in cohorts of students from one year to the next.[28] The Colorado student assessment program from 1997 to 2000 indicates that only about half the schools would meet even a one percentage-point proficiency gain or better in a single subject, even without requiring that all subgroups within the school meet the standard. Although NCLB expects schools to meet their AYP objectives each year, in fact many schools that meet the target in one year will fail to do so the next year. "Even with a single test and without separate subgroup reporting; only one school in twenty would have met the target increase three years in a row."[29]

Both measurement and sampling errors contribute to the volatility of scores. As in much of life, trade-offs should be considered. Averaging over large numbers will yield more-stable, less-volatile numbers but neglect the fine grain of subgroup analysis and disaggregated subjects and proficiency levels. Similarly, results averaged over several years may be less error-prone but less relevant for policy, merit pay, or other decisions in the latest year. On the other hand, who can argue with the goal of helping all children achieve proficiency in all subjects? As pointed out in the opening of this chapter, many schools with many students of lower socioeconomic status have made unexpected progress. Why not all?

Reporting Issues

Schools with large numbers of students that perform well on tests have been able to hide the poor results of a smaller number of students. NCLB provides such schools with a challenge: A school will be in trouble if only, say, 15 percent of its students with disabilities, or a group of minority students, are not meeting these same learning standards as the higher performing students.

Even so, in view of large gaps in achievement of poor, African American, Hispanic, and disabled students, NCLB has a "safe harbor" provision. If any subgroup's scores are below expected proficiency levels, the school may still attain AYP if 10 percent of the subgroup have gained proficiency since the last test. NCLB also "complements the provisions in IDEA (Individuals with Disabilities Education Act) by providing public accountability at the school, district and state levels for all students with disabilities" by requiring separate scores for disabled students.[30]

To obtain statistically reliable information (and to make sure that the identity of students in the subgroup is not publicized), each subgroup requires a minimum number of students to validate its achievement. An informal, unpublished survey of thirty-seven states found the required minimum number ranged from three to forty, with ten as the most common. Estimates based on samples of ten or less may be unstable; it may be reasonable to allow averaging the results over a two- or three-year period.

Students with disabilities are allowed accommodations when taking these state assessments. The student's Individual Education Plan team, including the parents, must determine these accommodations, which should be based on the student's individual needs and similar to those provided to the student during classroom assessment. Under NCLB, accommodations are defined as changes in testing materials or procedures to ensure that an assessment measures the student's knowledge rather than the student's disability.

Can a student's disability be so serious that he or she does not have to take the state assessment? Yes, but each state must have an alternative assessment in place for students who cannot participate in the typical test because of significant cognitive impairment. Those assessments may center on a portfolio approach tied to extended learning standards. This concept is consistent with the philosophy that all students can learn and the law that schools are accountable for their learning. The challenge for states is to overcome their relatively short histories of developing valid, reliable, and efficient assessments of severely disabled students.

Although well intentioned, subgroup provisions may entail unintended consequences. In the first place, they risk stereotyping students as group members rather than as unique individuals. In addition, the provisions are likely to have triage effects of overly concentrating attention and resources on some groups or individuals more than on others. Rational parents, disadvantaged by such policies and who care more about their own children than abstract egalitarian ideals may enroll their children elsewhere, which may contribute to economic and ethnic separateness and separatism.

National Assessment of Educational Progress

NCLB requires biennial participation in "state NAEP," which monitors state achievement trends. The law does not indicate which use, if any, will be made of the NAEP results. NAEP, however, is the best and perhaps the only valid common achievement measure that can serve as a benchmark for comparing states. The National Assessment Governing Board adopts its standards through a "broadly inclusive process."[31] The NAEP Mathematics Framework for 2003 states the following:

> The National Assessment of Educational Progress (NAEP) is the only nationally representative and continuing assessment of what America's students know and can do. It is a congressionally mandated project of the U. S. Department of Education's National Center for Education Statistics. NAEP measures student achievement in reading, mathematics, writing, science, U. S. history, geography, civics, the arts, and other subjects. Since 1969 NAEP has surveyed the achievement of students at ages 9, 13, and 17 and, since the 1980s, in grades 4, 8, and 12.
>
> In 1990, the U. S. Department of Education conducted the first voluntary state-by-state assessment as an adjunct to its periodic NAEP national assessments. . . . The 1990 state-level trial was limited to the 8th grade. In 1992, the second voluntary state-level assessments associated with NAEP were carried out at the fourth- and eighth-grade levels in mathematics and at the fourth-grade level in reading. Current NAEP legislation in the No Child Left Behind Act of 2001 requires that NAEP assess mathematics and reading every two years at the national and state levels in grades 4- 8. This schedule begins with the 2003 assessment."[32]

The NAEP Governing Board established several achievement levels to describe what students should know and be able to do. Those levels are as follows:

- *Basic* denotes partial mastery of prerequisite knowledge and skills that are fundamental for proficient work at each grade.
- *Proficient* represents solid academic performance for each assessed grade. Students who reach this level have

demonstrated competence over challenging subject matter, including subject matter knowledge, application of such knowledge to real-world situations, and analytic skills appropriate to the subject matter.

- *Advanced* represents superior performance.

Some students, of course, can be *below basic*, which means there are four groups of students. *Proficient*, however, is often taken as the chief standard that all students should meet.

Comparing National and State Proficiency

As reported by the Education Trust,[33] consistently fewer students met NAEP standards than their own state standards (see Table 3.2). One explanation is that schools geared instruction more toward state than toward NAEP standards. It is also possible that some states have relatively slack standards compared to NAEP, and that because some states have only recently begun participating in NAEP, they may not have geared up for it.

A panel of the National Research Council claims there is too much variability in state tests to justify attempts to equate them to each other or to NAEP at the student level.[34] "Relying on NAEP to determine performance levels would be problematic because of the stringency of the achievement levels—NAEP's performance standards."[35] For the 2000 NAEP assessments, for example, their calculations show that the number of students scoring at the proficient level or higher was 32 percent in reading at fourth-grade, 28 percent in math at eighth grade, 28 percent in fourth grade math, and 33 percent in reading at eighth grade.

One prominent test authority thinks that "NAEP performance standards are clearly ambitious, maybe too ambitious. Certainly the target of 100% proficient or above according to the NAEP standards by the 2013–14 school year appears more like wishful thinking than a realistic possibility. Yet the high jump bar is set at that height for every school and State."[36] He then projects how long such attainment might take. "Based on a straight-line projection of those rates of improvement, it would take 57 years for the percentage at Grade 4 to reach 100. For Grade 8 it would take 61 years and for Grade 12 it would take 166 years. In reading, it would take even longer to reach 100%."[37]

On the other hand, as noted earlier, accountability appears to be increasing rates of progress. In addition, U.S. students are far behind their Asian and European peers, notwithstanding the higher per-student costs of American schools. There is no reason that the United States cannot raise school productivity to or beyond the levels of other advanced countries. Clear and demanding goals, moreover, usually result in better results than vague, "do your best" goals. Better to aim for excellence at NAEP's high goals rather than at what some schools think is passable.[38]

The states themselves vary considerably in their goals or standards as to the percentages of their students that achieve proficiency (see Table 3.2). In fourth- and fifth-grade mathematics, for example, Texas finds 93 percent of its students proficient, Maryland only 42 percent.

The Education Trust argues that

We should resist the urge to compare states based on the number of schools that failed to make AYP this year. It's not a contest among states; it is a process for identifying individual schools and districts that need improvement. NCLB was specifically designed to let states make their own decisions

Table 3.2.   National and State Percentages of Students Proficient or Above

State	Fourth- and fifth-grade reading		Seventh- and eighth-grade mathematics	
	State	NAEP	State	NAEP
California	36	20	29	18
Florida	55	23	53	XX*
Georgia	74	24	58	19
Illinois	59	XX	53	27
Maryland	42	29	35	29
New York	59	29	41	26
North Carolina	77	28	82	30
Texas	93	29	93	24

* indicates state non-participation.

about what their children need to learn and how to assess that learning. Because of the central state and local role in education, AYP results don't allow apples-to-apples comparisons of student achievement from one state to another.[39]

Still, citizens pay for schools, and their representative legislators are in charge of collecting the data. All should have a right to see what the data say. It is useful, for instance, to know that New York spends much more than Montana yet has lower test scores. Citizens in both states may find this of keen interest, raise important questions, and determine what to do about it.

Multiple Indicators

If the recommendations made above are followed, tests in other areas would be added in the coming years to assess progress more comprehensively, at least in science and social studies, if not in the arts, music, and possibly other subjects. Rather than the generic social studies, it may be informative also to have separate reports and scores for history, geography, and civics or political science to be sure these subjects are given explicit attention.

Those and other similar additions to the basic information may present a problem of excessive data to report. Given, say, four subjects, four levels of proficiency (for example, below basic, basic, proficient, and advanced), and four grade levels would yield sixty-four pieces of data for each school. NCLB expands grade-level reporting to grades 3 through 8. It also requires separate reporting on economically disadvantaged students from major racial and ethnic groups, students with disabilities, and students with limited English proficiency.

Should a few, dozens, or hundreds of data points and comparisons be reported? Several principles of analysis and reporting may be useful. With the important caveat of preventing any risk of identifying a child, all data should be available to any person or institution for analysis and reporting. Yet providing too much data can be worse than providing none. Therefore, careful consideration should be given to making various levels and details of information for different groups.

For the public and legislators, only a few numbers for school and district trends may be best. Even one number—the percentage of proficient students averaged for the subjects and grades assessed—may best facilitate a comparison of schools and districts and compare those results with the goals for 2014, the year NCLB calls for all students to be proficient. On the other hand, school boards, educators, and parents might want fine-grain, even if less reliable, information on subgroups of students for various subjects and grade levels, and they want to see status scores and gains from year to year and even how the students of a particular teacher progressed.

Conclusion and Recommendations

The passage of NCLB legislation enjoyed presidential and bipartisan congressional support. Legislators and the executive branch appear motivated by the shared desire to improve the education of our nation's children and youth. NCLB relies heavily on testing and accountability requirements to promote substantial improvements in student learning. More and better information will be made available to legislators, educators, parents, and the public to identify strengths and weaknesses and provide direction in improving achievement.

Research has already shown the benefits of such efforts, and NCLB seems likely to magnify and extend them. If states continue to develop strong content standards, align tests to those standards, hold schools accountable for the achievement of all subgroups of students, and use the results for school improvement, substantial progress seems likely.

In continuing to implement NCLB, policymakers and educators face difficult but not insuperable problems. Several of the most important are discussed above, and those suggestions, along with time and further experience with the NCLB requirements, may help solve them. In conclusion, several recommendations for federal policies are worth enumerating and explaining:

1. *Stay the course; increase momentum.* The opening paragraphs of this chapter describe evidence that accountability works efficiently and well. It may lead temporarily or indefinitely to new and less comfortable consequences for school staff, but several recent nationwide studies show that it effectively and efficiently improves children's learning—which should be the main purpose of K–12 schooling. Both Democrats and Republicans strongly supported the initial legislation. To weaken the assessment requirements and standards now would show irresolution and cause enormous confusion at the state and local levels. The momentum should not be reduced but increased.

2. *Sponsor and convene state education policy and technical groups.* As we see in chart 1, some states have better met the goals of the NCLB legislation than other states. They developed ways to make the federal requirements and state priorities complement one another. Following the U.S. Department's peer review of state plans, opportunities for organized analysis and criticism of implementation plans are likely to continue benefiting state participants. (Although not a federal responsibility, states might convene within-state groups of districts and schools to share problems and breakthroughs.)

3. *Extend assessment coverage.* An exclusive focus on reading, language arts, and mathematics (and science in 2007) may lead to neglect of such important subjects as civics and history and such skills as writing. It is not premature to consider, plan, and schedule the incorporation of such subjects and skills into state assessments and NAEP testing requirements sooner than required.

4. *Commission assessment research including related state demonstration projects:*

   a. *Computer-adaptive and frequent tests:* Computer-adaptive tests save students' time and can yield nearly instantaneous results valuable to educators, parents, and students themselves. They allow tests to be given at will and frequently so that learning progress can be assessed more than once or twice a year. Computer-adaptive tests may be centrally revised and administered without the delay and expense of printing and two-way shipping.

b. *Parent and student surveys*: Although tests are the best single indicators of student and school success, they do not indicate all that education consumers may want to know about a school. For example, surveys show that many students feel insufficiently challenged; they and parents favor greater rigor. If choice is to prosper, partially because of NCLB, it will be valuable for parents to know such things as how welcome other parents and their children feel at alternative schools and their views of schools' features, strengths, and weaknesses.

c. *Incentives*: Although sufficient monetary and other incentives have huge effects on human behavior, oddly they are insufficiently acknowledged and employed in K–12 education. How can assessment best serve as the basis for various kinds of incentives for districts, schools, teachers, and students to raise achievement?

5. *For long-term study, consider the question of NAEP calibration with state assessment systems and NAEP as a possible substitute for parts or all of state assessment systems.* Countries with the highest school achievement typically have national standards, curricula, and assessments, which, in principle, enable educators anywhere in the country to know what students have studied in previous grades even if they move long distances. National examinations also enable legislators, citizens, and parents to examine student and school performance anywhere in a nation. Such a system, however, may threaten the American heritage of state and local control. What are the possible advantages and disadvantages for our nation's students?

Notes

1. Craig D. Jerald, *Dispelling the Myth Revisited* (Washington, D.C.: Education Trust, 2001).
2. G. Cawelti, "What Is Our Knowledge Base for Improving Student Achievement?" *Iowa Educational Leadership* 28 (2000): 3–8.
3. Martin Carnoy and Susanna Loeb, "Does External Accountability Affect Student Outcomes? A Cross-State Analysis," *Educational Evaluation and Policy Analysis*, forthcoming.
4. Caroline M. Hoxby, "The Cost of Accountability," in Williamson Evers and Herbert J. Walberg, eds., *School Accountability* (Stanford, Calif.: Hoover Institution Press, 2002): 47–74.
5. William Erpenbach et al., *Statewide Education Accountability under NCLB* (Washington, D.C.: Council of Chief State School Officers, 2003): 2. For brevity, reading here refers to all language arts.
6. Ibid., 6.
7. Ibid., 5.
8. Richard W. Cross, Theodor Rebarber, and Justin Torres (foreword by Chester E. Finn Jr.) *Grading the Systems: The Guide to State Standards, Tests, and Accountability Policies* (Washington, D.C.: Fordham Foundation, 2004): 13.
9. Education Commission of the States, *ECS Report to the Nation*, at http://nclb2.ecs.org/Projects_Centers/index.aspx?issueid=gen&IssueName=General.
10. Chester Finn, "The Marriage of Standards Based Reform and the Marketplace."
11. Martin Carnoy and Susanna Loeb, "Does External Accountability Affect Student Outcomes? A Cross State Analysis," *Education Evaluation and Policy Analysis* 24(4): 305-31.
12. "Standards and Tests: Keeping Them Aligned," *Research Points* (Washington, D.C.: American Education Research Association, spring 2003): 1.
13. Having many specific objectives and subobjectives may be less problematic. If the assessment makes no claim to measure each objective, as might a state that has three hundred detailed science objectives, then a sampling of student performance may suffice. This principle is analogous to social and political surveys that may sample only 1,000 people to estimate national views. The principle serves well in licensing tests in medicine, law, and other fields that cover broad, complex content. As in NAEP, random subgroups of students may be given random sets of times to estimate performance, but this

would exacerbate the problem of small sample size discussed in the text.

14. Lorrie Shepherd and K. Dougherty, "Effects of High Stakes Testing on Instruction," paper presented at the annual meeting of the American Educational Research Association, Chicago, April 1991. William Mehrens and J. Kaminski, "Methods for Improving Standardized Test Scores: Fruitful, Fruitless, or Fraudulent?" *Education Measurement: Issues and Practice* 8 (1) (Washington, D.C., 1989): 14–22.

15. Robert Linn, "Accountability: Responsibility and Reasonable Expectations," *Education Researcher* 32 (7) (Washington, D.C., October 2003): 4.

16. Erpenbach, *Statewide Education Accountability*, 9.

17. Ibid.

18. *Standards for Educational and Psychological Testing*, National Council on Measurement in Education, the American Educational Research Association, and the American Psychological Association (Washington, D.C., 1999).

19. Eva Baker and Robert Linn, "Validity Issues for Accountability Systems" (Center for the Study of Evaluation, Los Angeles, 2002): 4.

20. Standard 9.

21. Standard 17.

22. Linn suggests alternatives to the present system of the ever-increasing high bar. He suggests these considerations: longitudinal tracking of students from year to year; use of rolling averages across multiple years; the use of composite scores across subject areas and grades; use of separate grade by subject area results, through the setting of targets other than all combinations showing improvement (e.g., five out of eight, or seven out of ten possible grades by subject combinations). Why consider modifications? Because of the nature of these rising cut scores, a school that starts out very low (perhaps 20 percent proficiency) but makes great gains of 5 percent yearly for six years could be on a six-year watch list. However, a school that started very high (75 percent) but declined 2 to 3 percent annually for six years could be absent of any watch list.

23. Standard 19.

24. Thomas Kerins, ed., *Assessment Handbook: A Guide for Developing Assessment Programs in Illinois* (Springfield: Illinois State Board of Education, 1995).

25. Baker and Linn, "Validity Issues," xx.

26. Thomas Kerins, ed., *Assessment Handbook: A Guide for Developing Assessment Programs in Illinois* (Springfield: Illinois State Board of Education, 1995).

27. Standard 25; Standard 31.

28. Robert Linn and Eva Baker, "Accountability Systems: Implications of Requirements of the No Child Left Behind Act of 2001" (Center for the Study of Evaluation, Los Angeles, 2002), 17.

29. Ibid., 18.

30. "Accountability for Assessment Results in the No Child Left Behind Act: What It Means for Children with Disabilities" (National Center on Educational Outcomes, University of Minnesota, August 2003): 2.

31. http://nces.ed.gov/nationasreportcard/

32. Ibid.

33. Education Watch, "Achievement, Attainment, and Opportunity" (Education Trust, Inc., Washington, D.C., winter 2002-2003): xx.

34. Linn, "Accountability Systems," 20.

35. Ibid.

36. Linn, "Accountability: Responsibility," 21.

37. Ibid.

38. Herbert J. Walberg, "Real Accountability," in Paul E. Peterson, ed., Our Schools and Our Future . . . Are We Still at Risk? (Stanford, Calif.: Hoover Institution Press, 2003), 305–28.

39. Daria Hall et al., What New "AYP" Information Tells Us about Schools, States, and Public Education (Education Trust, Inc., Washington, D.C. 2003), 10.

4

Adequate Yearly Progress: Refining the Heart of the No Child Left Behind Act

Caroline M. Hoxby

No Child Left Behind (NCLB) aims to make every student in the United States proficient by 2014. Between now and that year, we need some way to judge whether schools are improving quickly enough to attain that goal. That is where adequate yearly progress (AYP), the annual standard that a school must reach to be judged on the right track, comes in.

The goal of making every child proficient is laudable, as is the commitment to get it done in real time. NCLB is on the mark in creating an annual standard against which schools can measure themselves; we cannot wait until 2014 to check on schools' performance. NCLB is also correct in insisting that schools make progress with subgroups of students who have lagged behind others in the past. Students who are disadvantaged minorities, non-native English speakers, poor, or disabled are further from proficiency now. If they have the longest way to go, schools need to focus on their progress now. Measuring the annual progress of subgroups will keep schools from spending the first few years under NCLB getting the easy cases past the proficiency bar and leaving the hard cases for last.

In short, not only is there merit in determining whether a school and subgroups of its students are making AYP, but so doing is the heart of NCLB. Unfortunately, although the principles and even much of the specific language for AYP are good, the implementation has been unnecessarily clumsy and sometimes unscientific. In this chapter, I suggest a way to implement AYP that is grounded in science, easy for schools to understand, unlikely to penalize schools arbitrarily, unlikely to induce states to dilute their notions of proficiency, and likely to get all schools on the path toward universal proficiency by 2014. Specifically, I suggest that:

1. States' proficiency standards should be benchmarked using the National Assessment of Educational Progress (NAEP).

   Such benchmarking will discourage states from reducing their proficiency standards by drawing attention to states that set low proficiency standards. Benchmarking will also give the U.S. Department of Education a *scientific* basis for deciding whether some states deserve extensions of the time to reach proficiency because they have set their proficiency standards significantly higher than those of the typical state.

2. AYP should be determined according to conventional statistical standards. Tests for AYP, the subgroup size, and the "moving window" (the number of recent years of achievement data) over which AYP is computed should not be set arbitrarily but should follow conventional statistical procedure.

   A school or subgroup should be judged to have failed to make AYP if conventional statistical tests reject the hypothesis that 100 percent of the school's or subgroup's students will attain proficiency by 2014.

   Using this method means that there will be no need to set an arbitrary subgroup size. In contrast, current implementation of NCLB allows states to compute AYP on subgroups that may be too small to be statistically valid.

   Each state examines a "moving window" to determine whether schools have made AYP. A state should set the length of its moving windows based on conventional statistical power calculations, which tell us how much data we need in order to test AYP.

3. AYP should not be mysterious. Schools should get projections of their achievement based on the statistics described above. Those projections should include a low, medium,

and high forecast of achievement and demonstrate *visually* why a school or subgroup is failing to make AYP.

4. Schools should be encouraged to have all students take state tests by calculating AYP as a "lower bound." To compute a lower bound, each nonparticipating student is factored in as though he or she had scored the minimum possible on the test.

    A lower bound calculation is statistically valid, amply rewards schools that maximize participation, and amply penalizes schools that fail to get full participation. In contrast, a 95 percent participation cutoff is an arbitrary way to determine whether a school is failing to make AYP.

5. The *yearly* in adequate yearly progress should be taken seriously: a student's achievement should not be fully factored into a school's AYP unless the student has been enrolled for at least 90 percent of the year since the last test was administered. However, if a student switches schools within a local education agency (LEA), his/her achievement should be factored into AYP with a weight equal to the share of the year that he/she spent in each school.[1]

The Spirit of Adequate Yearly Progress

Because the calculations are somewhat technical, it is easy to "lose the forest for the trees" when thinking about AYP. Let us consider the heart—the goals and spirit—of the AYP provisions. They are as follows.

1. The goal of AYP is to ensure that every school is on a trajectory such that all of its students will reach proficient achievement in a finite and relatively short number of years.

2. Because the goal is to make all students proficient, schools need to know if the trajectory of an identifiable subgroup of students makes them unlikely to achieve proficiency on time. The subgroups are the major racial groups, the economically disadvantaged, the limited English proficient, and the disabled.

3. Schools should be rewarded when a high percentage of their students participate in statewide testing. Schools should not be able to appear proficient by discouraging low achieving students from taking the tests.
4. States should have considerable freedom to set up their own systems of testing and accountability, both because education is largely a state responsibility and because states learn from other states' experiences.
5. All schools should achieve proficiency in both reading and mathematics.
6. Although states should feel free to add measures other than statewide tests to their accountability systems, no school or district that fails to make AYP on the basis of achievement results should be able to make AYP on the basis of other measures.
7. Schools are to be held accountable for the performance of students they educate, not for the performance of students they did not educate. Nevertheless, children who switch schools should not be neglected.
8. The 2013–2014 school year should be the deadline for reaching proficiency, at least for those states that have chosen typical (as opposed to unusually high) levels of proficiency.

Boiled down, AYP is simple: every student should be on a path that, if projected forward, will lead him to be proficient by 2014. The *every* is a core principle of NCLB: we must ensure that no group of students—minority, disabled, poor, limited English proficient, mobile—is left behind.

Another core principle of NCLB is that every child is capable of attaining proficiency, defined in an appropriate way. (States actually exercise considerable flexibility in determining proficiency for disabled and other special students.) NCLB deliberately emphasizes *reaching proficiency*, not just making gains every year. Its goal is to make every U.S-educated person capable of living in our modern society and economy. The consequence is that NCLB mainly scrutinizes the proficiency threshold, although it also (through the "safe harbor" provision) recognizes gains among students who are well below proficiency but making rapid progress toward it. NCLB provides no special recognition to schools where students start out proficient and subsequently attain more advanced learning. This is not a good thing or a bad thing but a choice about focus. The federal government has chosen to focus on bringing up low-achieving students. The states, with fewer schools to monitor, are in a better position to monitor multiple targets than is the federal government. States should be encouraged, in their own accountability systems, to reward schools that make gains along the entire spectrum of achievement.

Adequate Yearly Progress as It Was Meant to Be

The generalized language in the AYP provisions of NCLB is on the right track. The legislation says, in part:

Adequate yearly progress shall be defined by the State in a manner that (i) applies the same high standards of academic achievement to all public elementary school and secondary school students in the State; (ii) is statistically valid and reliable; . . . (iv) measures the progress of public elementary schools, secondary schools and local educational agencies and the State based primarily on . . . academic assessments. . . . (v) includes separate measurable annual objectives for continuous and substantial improvement for each of the following: . . . all public elementary school and secondary school students . . . economically disadvantaged students, students from major racial and ethnic groups, students with disabilities, and students with limited English proficiency; except that disaggregation of data . . . shall not be required in a case in which the number of students in a category is insufficient to yield statistically reliable information . . .

Each State shall establish a timeline for adequate yearly progress. The timeline shall ensure that not later than 12 years after the end of the 2001–2002 school year, all students in each group . . . will meet or exceed the State's proficient level of academic achievement on the State assessments.

However, actual NCLB rules do not always implement the generalized language. In particular, although the legislation repeatedly states that AYP assessment should be based on statistics that are valid, the regulations that help states abide by NCLB sometimes guide the states toward statistically invalid calculations. An invalid AYP calculation may show a school as failing when it is not. Such mistakes undermine the legitimacy of the law, not just among parents and teachers, but even among administrators and legislators who are proponents of accountability. In short, AYP can be substantially improved simply by aligning its regulations with its legislation.

In this chapter, I first consider the problem that the AYP regulations are trying to solve. Then, I show a conventional, valid statistical solution to the problem. It turns out that not only is the solution an improvement on current regulations, but it is also easier to implement and explain to administrators, teachers, parents, and concerned citizens.

Because NCLB respects states' and local governments' primary responsibility for overseeing and funding education, the legislation is silent on how states should set proficiency levels. Unfortunately, this silence set up a somewhat uneven playing field because, prior to NCLB, some states had set their proficiency levels much more ambitiously than others. Moreover, NCLB's silence on setting proficiency levels gives states perverse incentives to set (or reset) proficiency at modest levels so that AYP is achieved easily. The result is that the states most dedicated to improving achievement through accountability can be at a substantial disadvantage relative to the states that are lukewarm about accountability and are doing the minimum necessary to comply with NCLB.

In this chapter, I propose a solution to this problem that is workable but still allows states to maintain their independence. I show that it is feasible to benchmark each state's test against the NAEP. Benchmarking is a statistically valid basis upon which the Department of Education can adjust the deadline by which extra-ambitious states must attain proficiency.

Benchmarking States' Proficiency Levels

Ironically, the states that now take accountability the most seriously are penalized by NCLB because they set proficiency levels on the basis of their true judgment of what their students ought to know, not what their schools can readily achieve. NCLB never intended to pressure states into setting modest achievement targets. Rather, it was based on the assumption that states would tailor the standards to their circumstances but set proficiency levels in a fairly narrow range.

This assumption holds for the typical state, but what about the states that have set modest proficiency levels? Given that NCLB allowed all states to set proficiency levels and that part of its period of implementation has elapsed, the federal government must keep faith with them by sticking to their plans, which have already been approved. There is no reason, however, why their citizens should not be informed about the modesty of their proficiency goals. Such transparency will encourage states with modest standards to raise their proficiency levels, and discourage states with typical standards from lowering them.

What, however, can the federal government do to keep faith with states that set unusually high proficiency standards for themselves before NCLB was enacted? I propose that any state with a proficiency standard higher than the median state's standard should have its proficiency deadline extended in proportion to the amount by which its proficiency level exceeds the typical level. Such extensions will be meaningful only for states with a proficiency standard that exceeds the typical one by 8.3 percent or more, because each 8.3 percent corresponds to an extra year (one year is 8.3 percent of NCLB's twelve-year horizon), and extending the horizon by less than a year is not useful. Put another way, states that are only slightly more ambitious than the typical state will obtain no extension; extensions will be granted only to states that have set themselves an unusually hard task. Moreover, the basis of any extension will be clear and statistically valid, not arbitrary.

The key to making states' proficiency standards transparent is comparing them to a common benchmark. The only test administered to a representative sample of students in all the states is the NAEP, so it is the obvious candidate for the benchmark. Although NAEP is not a perfect bridge between states' tests, it is by far the best available.[2]

Matching percentiles is a statistically valid way to use NAEP to benchmark states' proficiency levels. To match percentiles, we need only determine the percentile that corresponds to each state's proficiency level. For instance, if 56 percent of a state's fourth graders are proficient, then the state's fourth-grade proficiency level is at the 56th percentile. We then examine the distribution of NAEP test scores for the same state in the same grade in the same year and find the NAEP score associated with the 56th percentile of the distribution. We have translated the state's proficiency level into NAEP points. (Indeed, we can easily translate not only states' standards for "proficient," but also their standards for "below basic," "basic," and "advanced.")[3] Once the translation is done for all the states, we can examine their proficiency levels against a common yardstick.

There is no way for NCLB to treat all of the states *identically* while still giving them autonomy and control over the schools that they largely fund. Nevertheless, the simple benchmarking I propose will encourage states with ambitious proficiency standards to keep them, expose proficiency standards are too modest, and inform political debates within the states themselves.

Implementing Adequate Yearly Progress in a Statistically Valid Way

The goal of the AYP provisions is to determine whether or not a school is on a trajectory to get 100 percent of its students to proficiency by 2014 (or an extended horizon, if it applies). This is a straightforward problem, statistically. This (the problem's straightforward nature) is a point that has been lost in recent discussions of NCLB. The task, however, is clear. We want to use a school's existing record of performance to forecast whether 100 percent of its students will attain proficiency by 2014. If our forecast is such that we can, using conventional statistical tests, reject the hypothesis that the school will attain proficiency by the deadline, then the school is failing to make AYP.

Moreover, using conventional statistical tests, we can determine whether a school is failing to make AYP because its overall progress is too slow or because we forecast that students in a particular subgroup will not attain proficiency.

Is a school forecast to attain universal proficiency in 2014? To answer this question, we can construct a linear forecast using a regression for each grade that is tested. Each student's information enters the regression as an observation, with the student's scale score being the outcome.[4] The explanatory variables are simply subgroup indicator variables, a time variable, and subgroup indicator variables interacted with the time variable. Each student's observation receives a weight equal to one, except that students who have been in a school for less than 90 percent of the year since the previous test should get a weight equal to the share of the year that they have been enrolled in the school. Below, I discuss how many years of data should be used for each school.

Having estimated this regression, we can forecast what each school's distribution of scores will be in 2014. Forecasts are not perfect, of course, and the uncertainty of each forecast is indicated by the standard error of the prediction. We can then compare the forecast scores to the proficiency level set by the state and ask what percentage of students we can confidently forecast to be below proficiency in 2014. In answering this question, we must take account of the uncertainty of the forecast. That is, we ought to be reasonably certain that students will fail to attain proficiency by 2014 before we state that a school if failing to make AYP.[5]

The regression described above will automatically generate the information we need in order to determine whether a school is making adequate yearly progress because one of its subgroups has disappointing growth in achievement. For instance, if the forecasts for economically disadvantaged students were such that we could confidently state that they would fail to attain proficiency by 2014, we would know that they were a source of the school's overall problem.

Thus, one benefit of this method is that it automatically shows a school failing to make AYP if students in one of its subgroups can be confidently predicted to be nonproficient. There is no need to choose a cutoff number at which a subgroup's performance starts to count. Instead, the standard error of the forecast automatically generates valid information about whether a subgroup is failing to make AYP.

Superficially, it may sound as though the test for whether a subgroup was failing to make AYP is much like current AYP provisions, under which a school fails to make AYP if one of its subgroups fails to do so. However, the test is not the same at all. The forecast for a subgroup is precise only if the subgroup has *systemically* poor achievement and achievement growth at a school. In such a case, the school will and *should* fail to make AYP. Current regulations encourage states to choose an arbitrary number of students above which a subgroup's performance counts, even if that number cannot support a valid statistical test of whether the subgroup is forecast to be proficient by 2014. Under current regulations, a subgroup may be shown as failing even though it is actually making AYP according to conventional statistics. This undermines the legitimacy of NCLB because a whole school can fail to make AYP because a single subgroup fails. Thus, a statistically invalid test is "spread" throughout a school and affects the whole.

A second major benefit of the method described above is that it automatically takes account of progress that students make toward proficiency, even if they do not cross the proficiency threshold. There is no need for a separate "safe harbor" provision. Even if a school's students start out far below proficiency, the school can make AYP by improving quickly enough that we forecast its being proficient by 2014.

A third major benefit of the method that I have described is that it provides a simple, fair way to allocate mobile students to schools. A school that educates a student for only a small share of a year will have that student's performance affect its forecasts by a proportionally small degree.

What a Typical Adequate Yearly Progress Report Ought to Look Like

A school's AYP report ought not to be mysterious. It ought to convey what it means to make adequate yearly progress—in other words, what it means for a school to be on-track or off-track toward the goal of universal proficiency. Thus, an AYP report should contain figures showing where the school is currently and where the school needs to be in the year 2014. The figures should show the best forecast of where a school will be in each year between the current year and 2014 and should indicate whether the forecast is precise or noisy. A figure ought to be created both for the school overall and for subgroups. Such figures can automatically be generated using the forecasts described above.

The figures I propose would look like figures that people often see in newspaper or business reports. They are easy to interpret and will help school staff understand why they are considered to be on-target or off-target. For instance, consider the following two figures, Figure 4.1 is for a school that is making

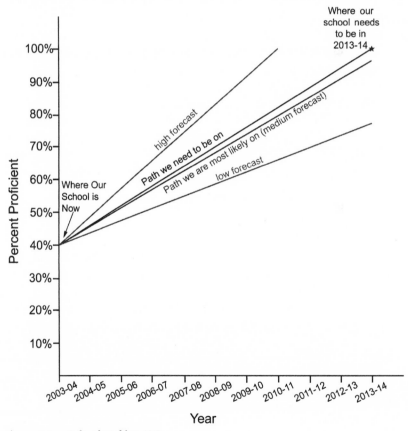

Figure 4.1. School Making AYP

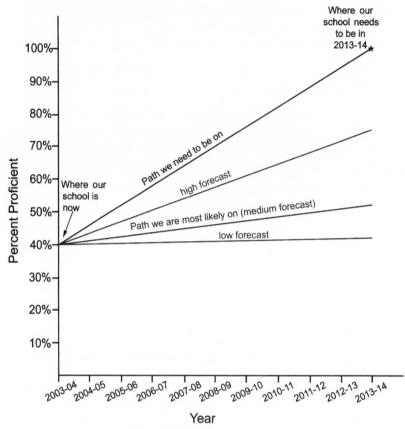

Figure 4.2.   School Failing to Make AYP

AYP but ought to do a bit better if it is going to continue to make AYP, and Figure 4.2 for a school that is failing to make AYP.

How Many Years of a School's Data Ought to Be Used for Adequate Yearly Progress?

If we use several years of past achievement data to make the forecast for each school, that forecast will be more precise. With a more precise forecast, we are more likely to identify a school that is failing to make AYP. Having multiple years of data is especially important for small schools because their small number of students in any given year will cause forecasts to be especially imprecise for them. On the other hand, if we use more years of data, the forecast will not reflect recent changes in a school's trajectory. For instance, if a school implements an outstanding new curriculum that improves its students' achievement, the new trajectory generated by the new curriculum will show up only in muted form in the forecast. We may continue to identify a school as failing to make AYP when it has already been turned around. There is a fundamental trade-off between the benefits of using more years of data (precision) and the costs (forecasts that do not sufficiently reflect recent changes).

How can a state resolve this trade-off? It must make a power calculation (a standard statistical computation). Essentially, the state must calculate, for schools of various sizes, how many years of data it needs to put in the regression in order to forecast confidently whether a school is making AYP. Once a state has made those power calculations, it can determine how many years of data it will use for each school. Unless a state's schools are all similar in size, the number of years should vary with a school's size, that is, a state should publish a schedule of school sizes and years of data to be used.[6]

Adjusting Adequate Yearly Progress for Participation

Under current legislation, a school fails to make AYP if fewer than 95 percent of its students participate in state assessments of achievement or if fewer than 95 percent of the students in any of its subgroups participate in assessment. (If a subgroup is too small for the AYP calculation, however, it is currently exempt from the participation requirement.) The goal of the participation provision is excellent. If we do not reward schools with high participation rates and penalize schools with low participation rates, then schools will have an incentive to discourage low-achieving students from participating in state assessments. Because making low-achieving students attain proficiency is the primary goal of NCLB, it would be counterproductive for the law to discourage their assessment. Nevertheless, NCLB's rule for factoring participation into AYP has no statistical basis and can thus arbitrarily cause schools to fail to make AYP.

NCLB's intention of encouraging full participation can be achieved in a simple and statistically valid way by computing a lower bound for each school's achievement. To compute a lower bound, each nonparticipant's achievement is entered into the regression described above as though he or she had scored the minimum possible on the state assessments. The school's lower bound can then be used to determine whether it has made AYP. Using the lower bound amply rewards schools that maximize participation and amply penalizes schools that deliberately exclude low-achieving students from assessments. After all, a low-achieving student can score no worse than the minimum possible, so having every child participate cannot worsen a school's chance of making AYP and would generally improve it significantly.

As a rule, regulations are more likely to create mistakes when they contain "knife-edges," like the 95 percent participation rule. A knife-edge occurs when a school can fail to make AYP because it has missed meeting a standard by only a tiny amount—which can happen for idiosyncratic reasons beyond a school's control. Whenever a regulation generates a mistake that seems obvious to everyone involved with a school, the legitimacy of the law is undermined.

Practical Refinements to the
Heart of No Child Left Behind

I have proposed refining the calculation of AYP in several ways, all of which move AYP toward the intention of the legislation. If the refinements were put in place, states would be less likely to lower their proficiency standards and more likely to raise them. The refinements would improve the statistical validity of AYP calculations and reduce the chance of a school mistakenly being classified as failing to make AYP. Moreover, the refinements would provide a statistical basis for making decisions that are currently made somewhat arbitrarily: the size that a subgroup must be before it is counted, the number of years of data used in the AYP calculation, the rate of participation that a school must achieve before failing to make AYP, accounting for the performance of students who switch schools. Finally, I believe that presenting AYP as a forecast will make it easier to understand what the law is all about.

AYP *is* the heart of NCLB. On it, many consequences of NCLB depend. Moreover, if the goal of NCLB—making every child proficient—is a correct one, then it is crucial to track whether we are on the path to achieving that goal. Refining AYP should be a key part of enhancing the usefulness and legitimacy of NCLB.

Notes

1. In states with longitudinal databases, students who switched schools within the *state* (not the LEA) should have their achievement allocated among the schools that educated them.

2. In particular, NAEP is not administered to students in all the grades that are required to be tested under NCLB. Tests in all grades are not necessary, however, simply for informing citizens and extending the deadline for states with unusually ambitious proficiency standards.

3. This method imposes almost no assumptions about the distributions of test scores. Statistically speaking, it is a highly nonparametric method of translating states' proficiency levels into a common standard.

4. A Tobit regression is appropriate because student progress above the proficiency level should not be used to predict the rate of progress of students up to the proficiency level. In a Tobit regression, scale scores above the proficiency level are capped at the proficiency level. Note that, if some group of students, such as the disabled, do not receive scale scores but are merely judged to be proficient or nonproficient, a probit regression should be used to make the forecast for them. A description of Tobit and probit regressions can be found in any good statistics or econometrics textbook.

5. The conventional confidence level used for such a test is 90 or 95 percent.

6. Sophisticated statistical forecasters tend to weight data accordingly to their recentness. Thus, the last school year's performance would receive the greatest weight, the second-to-last year's performance would receive the next greatest weight, and so on. Years in the remote past receive negligible weight. Sophisticated forecasters rarely set a moving window of a certain number of years, equally weight each year in the window, and completely ignore data outside the moving window. Because, however, it should be easy for school staff to understand the how each new year of performance contributes to AYP calculations, it is reasonable to set simple moving windows for the calculation of AYP.

5

Impacts and Implications of State Accountability Systems

Eric A. Hanushek

Adopting statewide accountability systems for schools has been one of the most striking reforms in American education policy in the past twenty-five years. The change in focus away from inputs and processes and toward outcomes marks a dramatic shift in orientation. The No Child Left Behind (NCLB) Act of 2001 pushed further toward accountability by requiring all states to develop accountability systems and by establishing a variety of performance requirements. This chapter draws on the experiences of state accountability systems introduced during the 1990s to suggest the potential of NCLB to improve the nation's schools.

Because of the newness of NCLB and because of its pattern of phase-in, it is not possible to ascertain the impact of the federal legislation per se. It is, however, possible to investigate the impact of state accountability introduced earlier. Because these state programs form the basis for much of the continuing response of the states, this strategy yields evidence directly relevant for current policy.

Investigation of state policies shows decisively that accountability leads to improved student performance. States implementing school accountability systems have seen student performance on the National Assessment of Educational Progress (NAEP) improve more than that in states not implementing accountability systems. Moreover, the improvements are concentrated in states that attach consequences to student results as opposed to those that merely report on performance.

Accountability systems aid all students, but there are different effects observed by racial and ethnic background. Hispanics gain most by the introduction of accountability as long as scores are disaggregated by race and ethnicity. African Americans, however, gain the least—implying that accountability will improve their scores but will also lead to a widened achievement gap with whites. This finding simply reflects the difficulty of meeting two different objectives with a single policy instrument.

The existing systems across the states, which form the basis for most state systems under NCLB, can be improved to get even better results. The most common approach for scoring schools aggregates students in ways that blur the precise role of school and nonschool factors. As a result, the accountability systems in most states offer rather blunt incentives. By moving the systems closer to ones that identify the value added of schools, and even of teachers, we could expect noticeably larger achievement results.

Background

States have always been the primary locus of education policy in the United States, adapting their programs to local circumstance and yielding a diverse array of programs across and within states. This context of state decision making implies that varieties of educational experiments are always being conducted. Indeed, in the case of school accountability, it is just this varied experimentation that permits an analysis of student impacts.

Starting in the mid-1980s many states in the United States voluntarily adopted accountability policies to measure the performance of their schools. These states began measuring the educational outcomes of their students and using these objective and external measures of performance as a way of gauging the effectiveness of their schools. The federal government entered into accountability with the No Child Left Behind Act of 2001, requiring all states to have comprehensive accountability systems in place by 2006. NCLB leaves many of the design details to states to decide, and states have naturally built on the general parameters for accountability that they had developed in earlier periods. Because of this continuation of state policies, understanding the impact of state accountability on student performance provides information that is directly relevant to assessing the impact of NCLB.

Indeed, it is not possible to evaluate NCLB per se at this time. Most important, the key provisions of NCLB are currently being phased in, thus providing little accumulated history of their impact. Additionally, although states are implementing the provisions of the law somewhat differently, the central provisions apply to schools across all states. As a result, it is difficult to develop a comparison group of schools that does not fall under the accountability statutes and that provides an indication of what would have happened without accountability.

On the other hand, states swift to adopt accountability can be contrasted with those that did not move as quickly toward that. Further, the performance of states that have adopted accountability measures can be contrasted with pre-adoption performance in those states. Thus, the variation in adoption allows us to analyze the impacts of accountability.

Understanding the impact of accountability is, however, complicated. Over the relevant period (as today), each state used its own testing instrument. And each state simultaneously differs in a variety of other ways. Thus, an analysis of accountability must be able to separate the effects of accountability from other factors that potentially affect student achievement.

Analyzing the Impacts of School Accountability

First, school performance must be measured on a consistent basis. An analysis of state differences is possible because of the extensive participation of states in the National Assessment of Educational Progress (NAEP), frequently referred to as the "nation's report card." In 1990 NAEP began a program of representative testing for states that volunteered to participate. Because students in all participating states take the same test, NAEP provides an independent and consistent measure by which to compare academic achievement across states—something not possible using the states' own tests. The influence of accountability policies can be discerned by tracking changes in NAEP cohort performance over time as state accountability systems are introduced.

Second, understanding the impact of such accountability must be put within the context of other state educational policies. This is particularly true for thinking about NCLB because the policy is designed to work within the basic federal system of education, where individual states are the primary decision-makers and where a substantial amount of state variation in design and testing is permitted. Both NCLB and state accountability operate within a larger world of other state policies and differences in state populations.

Analyzing the effects of accountability on student performance is difficult.[1] To begin with, because accountability systems are introduced across entire states, all local school districts in a state face a common incentive structure. Thus, the only possible variation comes from interstate differences in accountability, but, as noted, states also differ in ways other than accountability. Moreover, samples are further limited by the fact that a number of states did not participate in national testing programs, making even less information available.[2]

Our analytical strategy involves focusing on the performance of cohorts of students within each state. The NAEP assessed the performance of fourth- and eighth-grade students at different times. Because the testing protocol called for assessments at four-year intervals, the same cohort of students in each state can be observed at both fourth grade and subsequently eighth grade[3] (see Figure 5.1). Four different periods of NAEP growth across states (two for reading and two for mathematics) form the basic data for analysis.

Looking at growth in student achievement for each state implicitly accounts for major differences in state populations and state educational policies. Overall differences in states will enter

Figure 5.1.   State Testing in NAEP by Subject, Grade, and Year

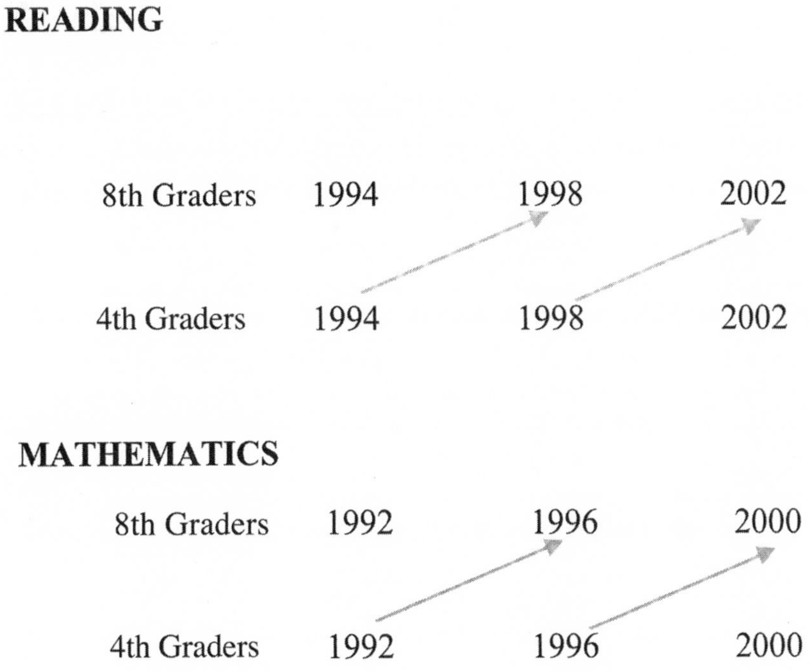

READING

| 8th Graders | 1994 | 1998 | 2002 |

| 4th Graders | 1994 | 1998 | 2002 |

MATHEMATICS

| 8th Graders | 1992 | 1996 | 2000 |

| 4th Graders | 1992 | 1996 | 2000 |

into fourth-grade performance. By considering the change in achievement from fourth to eighth grade, the focal point is factors that lead the pattern of achievement to change from what would be expected based on fourth-grade scores (and the basic state population and policy characteristics).

The key to this analysis is the introduction of accountability systems at varying times across states. Specifically, although a few states used accountability systems for schools in the early 1990s, the most significant expansion came later in the decade. Data on accountability come from a survey and analysis of all states by CREDO (the Center for Research on Education Outcomes, at the Hoover Institution).[4] For each state, information was collected on when a state introduced an accountability system for schools. For these purposes, an accountability system was defined as publishing outcome information on standardized tests for each school along with providing a way to aggregate and interpret the school performance.[5] States were classified by whether or not they attached consequences to school performance or simply provided a public report. Additionally, data were also collected on when a particular state began disaggregating test information by subgroups of the population. Note that these accountability measures pertain only to accountability for schools, not accountability for students that may have been introduced at a different time.[6]

The estimation relies on the varying timing of introduction of accountability systems into the different states. For the overall cumulative pattern of accountability across the states, see Figure 5.2. The data are broken up into states that attach consequences to their systems and those that simply report on school achievement. The NAEP testing dates for eighth-grade math and reading performance are superimposed on the pattern of accountability. The varied introduction across time and across the different testing periods permits us to disentangle the impact of accountability.

Finally, throughout the analysis, test results are disaggregated in white, African American, and Hispanic performance.

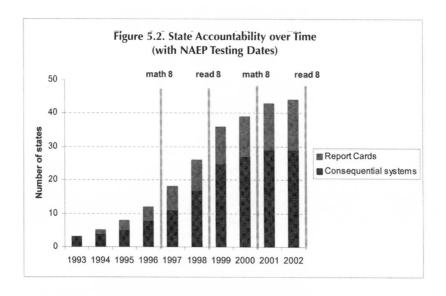

Figure 5.2. State Accountability over Time (with NAEP Testing Dates)

All the analyses rely on the pooled performance for each sub-group, and special attention is given to specific group differences.[7]

Effects of Accountability

The effects of introducing and employing school accountability systems are estimated from statistical models that also allow for other possible influences on achievement. From these statistical models, it is possible to separate accountability from other policies and from underlying differences in the populations of each state.

Accountability is important for students in the United States (and in other countries that are pushing for better performance measurements). Despite design flaws in the existing systems,[8] we find that they have a positive impact on achievement. This significantly positive effect of accountability holds across the alternative specifications of the basic achievement model.

The impact, however, holds only for those states attaching consequences to performance. States that simply provide better information through report cards without attaching consequences to performance do not get significantly larger impacts than those not having a formal accountability system. Thus, the NCLB move toward adding consequences to accountability systems is supported by looking at the historic introduction of consequential accountability systems.

It is useful to put the detailed subgroup impacts into perspective. The gains on NAEP scores (fourth to eighth grade) for whites, African Americans, and Hispanics are seen in Figure 5.3. By comparing the results in states without accountability and states with accountability, it is clear that introducing consequential accountability improves the performance of each group. On average, the white improvement is 0.21 standard deviations.[9] Further, accountability significantly increases the state achievement gain for minorities, particularly for Hispanics. However, because both African Americans and Hispanics show lower gains relative to whites on each of the tests, regardless of the availability of an accountability system, accountability by itself is insufficient to close the gap in learning.

The effect varies by subgroup, with Hispanics gaining most and African Americans gaining least (see Figure 5.4). Because whites gain more than African Americans after accountability is introduced, the achievement gap between those two groups actually widens with the introduction of accountability, while the achievement gap between Hispanics and whites declines.

The finding of differential effects of accountability raises a clear policy dilemma. A prime reason for the U.S. federal government to require each state to develop a test-based accountability system was simply raising the achievement of all students. These results suggest a beneficial effect on overall achievement but also indicate that some gaps across subgroups could widen. We conclude from this that additional policies are needed to deal with the multiple objectives. Again, as is frequently the case, a single policy cannot effectively work for two different objectives: raising overall student performance and providing more equal outcomes across groups.

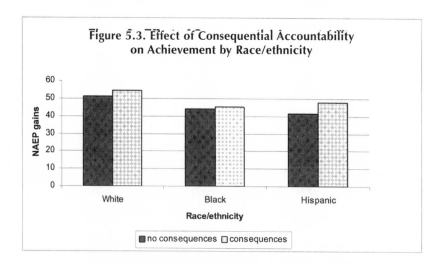

Figure 5.3. Effect of Consequential Accountability on Achievement by Race/ethnicity

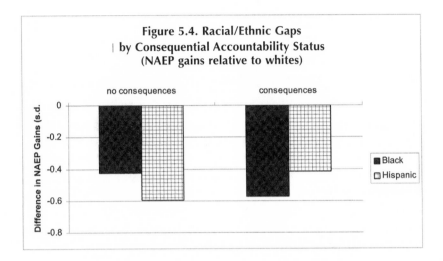

Figure 5.4. Racial/Ethnic Gaps
by Consequential Accountability Status
(NAEP gains relative to whites)

Importance of Student Achievement

Some people have questioned the basic foundation of state accountability. Specifically, many people suggest that skills measured on typical state tests are not very important for people after they leave school. These people generally go on to say that employers do not care about such measured skills, that other characteristics such as the ability to work well in teams are more important, and the like.

On this, a large body of work has assessed the economic importance of schooling and school quality. The simple answer from this work is that test performance is *very* important both for individual earnings and for the economic performance of the national economy.

Much of the early development of empirical work on the economics of schooling rightfully concentrated on the role of school attainment, that is, the quantity of schooling. This focus was natural. The revolution in the United States during the twentieth century was universal schooling. Moreover, quantity of schooling is easily measured, and data on years attained, both over time and across individuals, are readily available. Today, however, policy concerns revolve much more around issues of quality than around issues of quantity. The completion rates for high school and college have been roughly constant for a quarter of a century. Meanwhile, the standards movement in schools has focused on what students know as they progress through schools and the knowledge and skills of graduates.

Three U.S. studies provide direct and consistent estimates of the impact of test performance on earnings.[10] These studies employ different nationally representative data sets that follow students after they leave school and enter the labor force. When scores are standardized, they suggest that one standard deviation increase in mathematics performance at the end of high school translates into 12 percent higher annual earnings. There are reasons to believe that these estimates provide a lower bound on the impact of higher achievement.[11]

Another part of the returns realized from school quality comes through staying in school. Substantial evidence exists that U.S. students who do better in school, either through grades or scores on standardized achievement tests, tend to go further in school. Murnane et al. separate the direct earnings returns to measured skill from the indirect returns of more schooling and suggest that perhaps one-third to one-half of the full return of higher achievement comes from further schooling.[12] Note also that the effect of quality improvements on school attainment incorporates concerns about dropout rates. Specifically, higher student achievement keeps students in school longer, which leads, among other things, to higher graduation rates at all levels of schooling.

The relationship between labor force quality and economic growth is perhaps even more important than the impact of human capital and school quality on individual productivity and incomes. Economic growth determines how much improvement will occur in the overall standard of living of society. Moreover, the education of each individual has the possibility of making others better off (in addition to the individual benefits just discussed). Specifically, a more educated society may lead to higher rates of invention; may make everybody more productive through the ability of firms to introduce new and better production methods; and may lead to more rapid introduction of new technologies. These externalities provide extra reason for being concerned about the quality of schooling.

An analysis of growth rates across countries indicates that the quality of the labor force as measured by math and science scores is extremely important. One standard deviation difference on test performance is related to 1 percent difference in annual growth rates of gross domestic product (GDP) per capita.[13] This quality effect, which sounds small, is actually very large and significant. Because the added growth compounds, it leads to powerful effects on national income and on societal well-being. Indeed, some estimates indicate that true reform of U.S. schools (i.e., reforms that would lead to improved student achievement) could yield growth dividends that would be sufficient to pay for all of our current expenditures on K–12 education.[14]

In sum, these analyses demonstrate that improvements in schooling outcomes—of the type currently measured by state tests—are likely to have powerful impacts on individuals and on the economy as a whole. Although other aspects of schooling outcomes may also be important, there is no denying the clear relevance and importance of the skills measured by current tests.

Designing Accountability Systems

The obvious reason that accountability systems affect outcomes is that they provide incentives for schools to improve. Through providing better information and through attaching rewards or punishments to the outcomes, they encourage both students and school personnel to focus on improving student outcomes.

At the same time, incentives are superior when they focus attention on the things that individuals control. Most of the existing state systems do this imperfectly. Specifically, they rely on aggregations of individual student performance that do not accurately distinguish between the impact, or value added, of school from that of other factors. It is well known, for example, that families have a powerful effect on student learning. Thus, the average test score for all the students in a school will include not just the impact of teachers and schools but also the impact of families, friends, and neighborhoods.

A majority of the existing state systems concentrate on overall levels of school performance.[15] This is natural, because the goal of individual states and of the federal government in NCLB is to make sure that all students reach high levels of performance. Thus, they concentrate on the levels of performance for all students.

At the same time, such systems do not provide the strongest incentives for the individuals in the schools. Specifically, it is not always possible to separate out and reward the contribution of the school in any precise way. This inaccuracy in measurement (for the purpose of incentives) lessens the impact of the accountability system.

Existing state systems frequently modify the focus on average scores (or aggregate passing rates on tests) by focusing on changes over time for each school. Such a procedure is often motivated by an interest in focusing on school improvement (and, as discussed below, is indeed codified in NCLB under the requirements that schools make adequate yearly progress or AYP). Such a focus on changes in school performance over time partially helps separate the value added of schools from the influences of families, neighborhoods, and other nonschool influences. Unfortunately, because of student mobility across schools and differences among cohorts of students, this approach proves to be an unreliable way to isolate the separate effects of schools. Research investigating the relationship between the level of student achievement and the value added of schools shows that the rankings of schools can be dramatically affected by this problem.[16] Although there are ways of dealing with the problems, many common modifications employed by states remain problematic.

The precise impact, of course, depends on the details of the systems in individual states. But it appears that existing systems could be improved.

A second concern involves measures that relate to specific passing scores on tests. By concentrating on whether or not students are brought above each state's chosen level of proficiency, the accountability system places a huge emphasis on students who are near the passing level—and much less on those who are either significantly below or significantly above that level. For instance, when states set demanding standards with high levels of performance required, such schools can make exceptional progress without that progress being recorded. Specifically, students who are very unprepared—indeed just the students who are the focus of most policy concern—can experience substantial growth in learning without reaching proficiency levels. The strongest incentives would recognize these gains. The opposite is also the case. If a school has exceptionally well-prepared students—ones that begin above state proficiency levels—the school's actions may not be rewarded or sanctioned. Thus, the school may not provide much in the way of value added and may escape notice. A similar occurrence would result from a state's having either a very easy test or a very low cutoff for passing the test, where value added at the upper end does not show up in the accountability measures. This may also lead to less political support for accountability by parents of high-achieving students because they see the accountability system as being irrelevant and a distraction.

One obvious way to deal with both problems is to identify the growth in achievement of individual students. By following the performance of individuals, and by basing rewards at least partially on student gains in achievement, incentives can focus much more directly on the portion of achievement that schools are responsible for. Moreover, in such a system, more weight can be placed on performance at the bottom of the distribution, thus continuing the pressure on schools to ensure that everybody meets some minimum level.

The two problems can also be dealt with separately. For example, by requiring school gains at multiple points in the test performance scale, attention can be redirected to more than just the students near the passing mark. The imprecision of comparing performance across cohorts of students would, however, remain and would still lessen incentives unless dealt with in some manner.

An extension of this gains approach would actually take the measurement of performance down to the individual classroom level. Specifically, by linking individual teacher performance with student performance, it would be possible to provide rewards for high-quality teachers. This approach, which has been advocated in other contexts, would fit naturally within an accountability system that emphasized incentives for the participants.[17]

The notion of including individual student growth in calculating accountability measures relates directly to some of the more discussed aspects of No Child Left Behind, including the calculation of AYP. Although AYP has a natural relationship to ideas of growth and improvement, it can be complicated both by comparing different groups of students and by the interaction with the choice of proficiency levels. By insisting that individual students perform better over time, this important goal and check on performance is brought directly in line with the students of each school.

Many states do not have the capacity to follow individual students or to trace their performance. Nonetheless, it is possible to correct for mobility by a simple adjustment in the calculation of school aggregates. Specifically, by recording scores only for students who were present in the school at the prior year's testing, the change in aggregate scores across years provides the correct information on school value added. This approach does take a number of students out of the calculations for individual schools, but they can be included in district averages as long as they move within a district.[18]

A closely related issue has to do with the possibility of unintended consequences from the introduction of accountability systems. A variety of researchers and policy analysts have suggested that accountability systems can encourage schools to "game" the system (i.e., to behave in ways designed to improve measured outcomes without changing actual results). This problem appears generally to be overstated.[19] Nonetheless, some behavior certainly has such gaming in mind, and is made possible and reinforced by the kinds of inaccuracies in measurement discussed here. If the performance of individual students is not measured accurately, it is easier to pursue unproductive paths (that have the effect of improving just-measured outcomes). For example, if schools tend to keep students out of the testing program for strategic reasons, measured school performance can be improved without actually improving the performance of any students. But following individual students ameliorates such issues.[20]

Each of these issues points to more precise measurement of the achievement of individual students. The focus of ensuring high achievement for all can indeed be met by concentrating on individual students.

These considerations actually reinforce the strength of accountability systems for improving performance. Even though many state accountability systems are blunt instruments that do not precisely identify the value added of schools, they have had the powerful effects previously identified. This fact strongly suggests that added refinement will lead to substantial additional rewards.

Conclusions

The available evidence indicates clearly that state accountability systems are providing a powerful force to improve student achievement. Although this is not a direct investigation of the new elements of No Child Left Behind, it is clearly relevant, because the state responses to NCLB are a direct outgrowth of earlier experience with accountability systems.

The past evidence also indicates that the impact of accountability is directly related to its having consequences. Merely reporting the results of student outcomes does not yield the same strong effects. Thus, the inclusion of consequences in NCLB is warranted if we are to achieve the results that we desire.

At the same time, NCLB does not do everything we might want. Although accountability raises all performance, it has done so unevenly. Experience suggests that Hispanic achievement has responded most strongly to disaggregated accountability. White students have responded less than Hispanics but more than African American students. As a result, although accountability works to close the Hispanic-white gap in achievement, it does the opposite in terms of the gap between whites and African Americans.

The fact that accountability by itself does not meet all objectives should come as no surprise. When there are multiple objectives, it is generally not possible to achieve the desired results with a single policy instrument. Thus, improving overall achievement levels and simultaneously narrowing racial and ethnic gaps will require additional policies.

Finally, many state accountability systems could be improved by tightening the focus on the value added of schools. This can be done most effectively by following the growth of individual students or by focusing on students who are present across two consecutive testing periods. Relating student growth in performance to schools, and perhaps individual teachers, offers a clear way to improve the (already good) results of school accountability systems.

Notes

1. The discussion here summarizes the analysis in Eric A. Hanushek and Margaret E. Raymond, "Does School Accountability Lead to Improved Student Performance?" *Journal of Public Policy Analysis and Management* 24, no. 2 (spring 2004). That source provides the details of the statistical analysis underlying the discussion here.

2. A final issue considered in the empirical analysis involves NAEP test exclusions. Although testing is designed to cover a random sample of the student population, various exclusion rules are applied for special education students and for limited English proficient students—and the application of these rules has changed over time. The statistical analysis considers the impacts of this, but because it does not directly affect the accountability of estimates, it is not emphasized here. See Hanushek and Raymond, "Does School Accountability Lead to Improved Student Performance?"

3. Note that these are not the same identical students. Nonetheless, because the cohorts have many similar experiences, following cohorts permits implicitly controlling for a number of policies and other common elements.

4. Stephen H. Fletcher and Margaret E. Raymond, "The Future of California's Academic Performance Index," Center for Research on Education Outcomes, Hoover Institution, Stanford University (April 2002).

5. The survey further collected information on the method by which schools aggregated scores. The alternative approaches are discussed in Eric A. Hanushek and Margaret E. Raymond, "Lessons about the Design of State Accountability Systems," in *No Child Left Behind? The Politics and Practice of Accountability*, eds. Paul E. Peterson and Martin R. West (Washington, D.C.: Brookings Institution, 2003): 127–51.

6. See Martin Carnoy, and Susanna Loeb, "Does External Accountability Affect Student Outcomes? A Cross-State Analysis," *Educational Evaluation and Policy Analysis* 24, no. 4 (winter 2002): 305–31. They employ an index of intensity of accountability that covers both school and student accountability measures but do not consider differential times of introduction.

7. See Hanushek and Raymond, "Does School Accountability Lead to Improved Student Performance?" The detailed specifications that they describe separate growth estimates (fixed effects) for each state, time varying state spending and state parental education levels, exclusion rates for special education and limited English proficiency students, and disaggregated accountability by race.

8. Hanushek and Raymond, "Lessons about the Design of State Accountability Systems."

9.. These calculations rely on the standard deviation of average scores across states and subgroups for the eighth-grade performance, which equals 16.2 scale score points.

10. Casey B. Mulligan, "Galton versus the Human Capital Approach to Inheritance," *Journal of Political Economy* 107, no. 6, pt. 2 (December 1999): S184–S224. Richard J. Murnane, John B. Willett, Yves Duhaldeborde, and John H. Tyler, "How Important Are the Cognitive Skills of Teenagers in Predicting Subsequent Earnings?" *Journal of Policy Analysis and Management* 19, no. 4 (fall 2000): 547–68. Edward P. Lazear, "Teacher Incentives," *Swedish Economic Policy Review*, 2003.

11. First, these estimates are obtained fairly early in the work career (mid-twenties to early thirties), and other analysis suggest that the impact of test performance becomes larger with experience. Second, the labor market experiences that are observed began in the mid-1980s and extended into the mid-1990s, but other evidence suggests that the value of skills and of schooling has grown throughout and past that

period. Third, future general improvements in productivity are likely to lead to larger returns to skill.

12. Murnane et al., "How Important Are the Cognitive Skills of Teenagers in Predicting Subsequent Earnings?"

13. The details of this work can be found in Eric A. Hanushek and Dennis D. Kimko, "Schooling, Labor Force Quality, and the Growth of Nations," *American Economic Review* 90, no. 5 (December 2000): 1184–1208. See also Eric A. Hanushek, "The Importance of School Quality," in *Our Schools and Our Future: Are We Still at Risk?* ed. Paul E. Peterson (Stanford, Calif.: Hoover Institution Press, 2003): 141–73.

14. Eric A. Hanushek, "Some Simple Analytics of School Quality," National Bureau of Economic Research, Working Paper 10229 (January 2004).

15. For a more detailed description of alternative approaches along with the current distribution across schools, see Hanushek and Raymond, "Lessons about the Design of State Accountability Systems."

16. Eric A. Hanushek, Margaret E. Raymond, and Steven G. Rivkin, "Does It Matter How We Judge School Quality?" paper presented at American Education Finance Association annual meetings, March 11–13, 2004, in Salt Lake City.

17. For a discussion of alternative measures of teacher performance and of alternative reward systems, see Eric A. Hanushek and Steven G. Rivkin, "How to Improve the Supply of High Quality Teachers," in *Brookings Papers on Education Policy 2004,* ed. Diane Ravitch (Washington, D.C.: Brookings Institution): 7–44.

18. The concern is that schools serving disadvantaged students frequently have above-average mobility rates and thus would exclude a large number of students at the school level. However, the district can still be held responsible by aggregating scores for all students in the districts since the last testing.

19. Hanushek and Raymond, "Lessons about the Design of State Accountability Systems."

20. NCLB does provide a variety of regulatory safeguards to protect against such things as keeping certain students out of testing. The regulatory approaches are nonetheless difficult to set in ways that do not have commensurate unintended consequences. Thus, a movement to individually based gains can lessen many of the related problems.

6

Fixing Failing Schools in California

Williamson M. Evers and Lance T. Izumi

By passing the 2001 No Child Left Behind (NCLB) Act, the U.S. Congress changed the dynamics of school performance and created a new impetus to fix failing schools. Poorly performing schools now had to improve or they would be labeled failures and hit with sanctions. In the face of this new reality, states must figure out how to fix hundreds, even thousands, of poorly performing schools. Under NCLB and California's own accountability system, state officials expect to have large numbers of schools needing major improvement. As of early 2004, California's accountability system had designated forty-four California schools as failures. The state school board, having reviewed past efforts at school improvement, has devised a new system for fixing failing schools.

Under NCLB, California and other states judge their schools as successes or failures based on how well students do on standardized tests. In California, the test results used in such judgments are a combination of a commercially available, national norm-referenced test and a California test based on the state's own academic content standards, with the emphasis on results from the California standards-based test. Each state must set forth grade-level expectations for its students and a path of progress for its schools. School performance and progress are monitored.

If a school is not making "adequate" progress two years in a row, the state must place the school on its "needing improvement" list—in essence marking them as failures—until they improve. Not only must the students be making progress, but so must specified subgroups of the students (broken out by race, language, sex, and income).

The local district must offer students who are attending a school on he needing improvement list a choice of other public schools to attend. Failing schools must also offer extra services to students, including private tutoring. States can subject a failing school to a variety of sanctions, including a possible takeover or restaffing by the state after the sixth year.

Because of NCLB, California now has two parallel accountability systems. In the summer of 2003, the state submitted to the federal government its consolidated accountability plan based on the requirements of the federal law. California also continues to operate its separate state accountability system that predated NCLB. Although both systems are based mainly on student scores on the state's standardized tests, the two systems use these results differently. The federally required system looks at the progress of student achievement (i.e., the percentage of students at a school that reach a certain level of achievement as they progress toward the ultimate goal of scoring at the proficient level on the state test). In contrast, the state's system focuses on the performance growth of schools, not students, and measures that growth against an absolute scale. Both systems have developed somewhat similar intervention and sanction methods for dealing with underperforming schools.

Rigorous academic content standards are the basis of California's school accountability system. Rated as among the best in the country by education research organizations such as the Thomas B. Fordham Foundation, the state standards lay out and describe what students are expected to know in a variety of subjects at every grade level. The state's curriculum and textbooks, testing system, on-the-job teacher training (professional development), and school improvement program are all aligned to the standards.

In California, failing schools are identified by criteria contained in the state's school accountability system, created in 1999.[1] That system uses a measure called the Academic Performance Index (API) to calculate a schoolwide score between 200 and 1,000, based on student results on state tests at each school. The state board of education set 800 as the scoring goal; thus, schools scoring below 800 are required to meet annual growth targets based on a 5 percent increase over the school's current score. The API also ranks schools on a one-to-ten scale (ten being the best) on the basis of student test scores.

To address the problems of the schools that need improvement, California has created a series of interventionary programs. First there was the Immediate Intervention/Underperforming School Program (II/USP); then, High Priority Schools Grant Program (HPSGP). Participation by underperforming schools in both the II/USP and the HPSGP was voluntary. Now, as part of these programs, there is the School Assistance and Intervention Team (SAIT) approach, which can be imposed after two years of poor performance. As these programs have come into existence, the older ones have continued to run, while the new ones have influenced the practices undertaken in the continuing programs. Also, in these efforts, funding has come to concentrate, as the programs have developed, on the schools at the bottom levels of performance.

The successive interventionary programs echo, not accidentally, the preliminary corrective action plans of the NCLB Act. *Preliminary* because the programs do not include the harshest ultimate remedies (outsourcing, total restaffing, state takeover). From 1999 to 2003, failing California schools went through the first two phases (II/USP and HPSGP) of this school rescue progress. But independent scholars found that the process had negligible effects on student performance because the evaluation teams gave schools divergent and idiosyncratic recommendations. The recommendations usually emphasized classroom processes and school operations rather than what teachers are teaching and how effectively. After these initial years, failing schools continued to fail, and their students did not learn.

California officials learned from these programs' failure and thus established the SAIT approach, which takes direct aim at reading and math performance, rather than the scattershot approach of earlier interventions. SAIT stresses good management by the district and the school principal, aligning instruction with state academic standards and effective teaching of subject matter content. Because the SAIT approach is new, it is too soon to know whether it works; only anecdotal (but favorable) reports are available.

The open-ended provisions of the national NCLB law encourage states such as California to experiment with remedial action, an open-endedness consistent with America's federal system. But the law also sets down a six-year cycle of sanctions and expectations that failing schools will reach full proficiency by 2014. As time goes on, Americans will discover whether this situation combines flexibility with time pressures or is instead a recipe for disaster.

California's intervention programs are complex. For example, in the Immediate Intervention/Underperforming Schools Program, not all eligible low-performing schools became part of the intervention program. Participation was voluntary; to participate, schools had to apply. Schools that did apply and were selected then entered the program. Under II/USP, schools in the first year received $50,000 planning grants to develop a comprehensive school reform plan. As part of the planning phase, schools had to hire qualified external evaluators to assist in developing the improvement plans. The plans then had to be approved by the state board of education. After approval, the schools received annual implementation grants of up to $200 per enrolled student. Schools received the implementation grant for two years and could be granted a third year of funding if they continued to struggle to meet their academic performance index targets.

From 1999 until 2003, California had an "audit" program for external evaluators and school improvement plans, intended to be tailored to the flaws at each school.[2] The program included authorized evaluators of school improvement services and an official binder of suggested improvement projects. California chose not to depend on its own state department of education as its evaluator, instead relying on approved contractors, such as universities, private consulting firms, federal regional educational laboratories, and county offices of education. If a school was in trouble, it would choose a contractor, who would send out an observation team. The team would look at what teachers were doing in their classrooms in the failing school. Then the team, working with the school's teachers, would draw up a plan, perhaps making use of something in the binder of improvement projects.[3]

For example, the Los Angeles County Office of Education has a Division for School Improvement that offered assistance to failing schools and districts. "External evaluators" would assist a school by identifying problems "through classroom observation and data analysis" and then "work collaboratively" with a school's "action plan team" on solving them.[4]

But the pre-2004 approach wasn't working. A June 2003 study of the II/USP program found that, against "the backdrop" of very large increases in California's standards-based tests in the state, the "direct additional contribution" of the pre-2004 II/USP and related programs was "negligible."[5] That same study found serious weaknesses in the planning process for school improvement:

> Our case study data indicate a strong association between instructional coherence and growth in student achievement, while both case study and survey data reveal substantial variation among schools in their ability to develop a coherent instructional program. The planning process alone did not have a discernible influence on the development of instructional coherence.[6]

The pre-2004 approach in California had a built-in bias in favor of process rather than content. But the standardized tests measure student knowledge of academic content. A classroom-observation team can see teaching in practice; it can look at some lesson plans; it can learn about school procedures for helping faltering teachers. On the other hand, it is difficult for a visiting team to discover just what academic content is omitted over an entire year of teaching. In addition, the state did not have the resources to evaluate separately the teaching practices of all the teachers in hundreds, perhaps thousands, of schools.

In a situation where accountability measure are largely based on test scores and where standardized tests evaluate student knowledge, critics would look at these school improvement plans and ask, "Where's the content?" Critics asked of the classroom-observation teams, "When you look, what are you looking for?" Critics derided the state's binder of school improvement projects as "a hodgepodge," with suggested projects "totally unconnected" to the state's academic standards. In the hyperbolic words of one critic, the old approach had "180 million different ways" to fix schools but was unsystematic.[7] Many suggestions from the observation teams were, in the words of one critic, "off the wall"—for example, a recommendation that teachers undergo 350 hours of training.[8] In practice, the pre-2004 way, by focusing on the school as the only unit of change, kept local districts out of the school-improvement effort. California relied on exploratory, observational teams, but—naturally enough—their suggestions diverged from one another. Each school team was a boutique effort. There were no statewide measures of school behavior to check on actual improvement efforts. There was, in reality, no statewide system for improving schools that were in trouble.

In a time of educational reform that relies on standards and accountability, observation teams have to prove their worth as a principal way of diagnosing school needs. How can a visiting observation team do a better job of evaluating a school's problems than tests are already doing? Test results show the gaps in teaching content. A prearranged or an unexpected classroom observation may by chance detect content flaws in a lesson plan. But a more systematic approach would analyze a school's or a classroom's achievement as reflected in test results on specific questions or clusters of questions to locate gaps in coverage. It would then use content specialists to assist teachers in improving.

If classroom observation is meant to improve student achievement on a standards-based curriculum, it should not stand alone or be at a statewide level but rather be part of teacher training and school management.[9] Classroom observers (often school principals), working carefully, can at the school and district level help train teachers and evaluate how they are doing.

But like portfolios of classwork, once classroom observation is elevated to a statewide level, it breaks down. There is not enough time for careful observation, and the system loses sight of the particularities of the situation. When it comes to accountability, the state already knows from test results which schools are failing. In this context then, some want to use outside observers to diagnose what is weak or missing and to prescribe a cure (retraining teachers and specifying what should be done instead).

But classroom observations can too easily be subjective. Their weaknesses are similar to those of authentic assessment of student performance (i.e., classroom observations are unreliable, expensive, and time-consuming). Part of that unreliability is that teachers do not behave normally when they are being observed for evaluation.[10]

Classroom observations are also often inaccurate, with observers looking for the wrong things. Classroom observation as a basis for diagnosis and prescription lends itself too easily to bias. For example, if the classroom observers are traditionalists, they will note an absence of traditional practices and prescribe introducing them. If they are progressives, they will prescribe progressive practices. For instance, the state of Pennsylvania asked professors from the University of Pennsylvania's Graduate School of Education to help improve some failing Philadelphia schools. The professors (advocates of progressive education), after walk-throughs and observations in every classroom, prescribed enhancing the level of critical thinking in all teaching, increasing the emphasis on "big ideas" and problem solving in teaching math, and increasing the emphasis on inquiry in teaching science. Polished lessons in a teacher-led classroom were considered a ruse—a distraction from an ideal of constant improvisation in which teachers were to see themselves and their students as exploring and learning together. "A school climate becomes," according to these professors, who are here using the "constructivist" jargon of progressive education, "more productive when we all see ourselves as observers of, and contributors to, the myriad ways that learning can be constructed."[11]

Indeed, teachers who are undergoing observation will often try to learn the pedagogical preference of the observer. Then the teachers will teach the lesson to be observed in line with the observer's preference. This technique is common enough that it has a name: "the chameleon strategy."[12]

Without statewide common measures of school behavior to check on actual improvement efforts, some schools neglect to buckle down to the hard work of school reform. For example, the Education Commission of the States suggests that:

> low-performing schools and districts frequently focus on the form of improvement planning, such as holding meetings, rather than the substance, such as focusing on goals for student improvement, gathering data to examine progress toward those goals, and providing supports and pressures so that teachers meet those goals.[13]

Unfortunately such form-over-substance practices can be masked—for a while—by razzle-dazzle reporting. We want to fix failing schools so that children can learn. But under California's pre-2004 approach, school improvement did not concentrate on teachers' mastering the subject matter and delivering that subject matter to students so that they learned it. State officials had already detected this problem by 2000, although the old approach continued through December 2003. In November 2000, the California Education Policy Seminar and the California State University Institute for Education Reform held a conference on the first year of the Immediate Intervention/ Underperforming School Program, at which California secretary for education John Mockler reviewed the school improvement plans around the state. He said, "There was no discussion of curriculum. And there was very little mention of standards, so it was difficult to tell what the plans were really talking about."[14]

In the pre-2004 reform plan process, external evaluators made recommendations, but there was no third-party quality control over what those recommendations were. The State Board of Education was permitting groups to do things, but it had no idea what those things were. The assumption was that if one sent out evaluation teams, they would know what to do to fix the schools. Some school personnel complained that the external evaluators did little except put the ball in the court of teachers and principals to come up with a reform plan. Proponents of solid education complained that all too many evaluators recommended progressive student-centered teaching methods, such as discovery learning, that, according to empirical evidence, do little to improve student achievement.

Perhaps the most damaging criticism of the external evaluations, however, is that they often did little to ensure that low-performing schools implemented standards-based instruction and reform. The pre-2004 II/USP action plan for Central Valley Union High School (not its real name), the oldest high school in one of the counties in California's Central Valley, is a case in point. The district superintendent and school officials reviewed the portfolios of various external evaluators and then contracted with the UCLA Anderson School of Management to provide the external evaluation team (EET). The UCLA EET stressed process, holding meetings with the faculty to raise their awareness and understanding of the process, collecting data on the faculty's hopes and fears of the process, and holding a general meeting with parents, teachers, and administrators. The UCLA EET engaged in classroom observation, interviewed teachers and students, reviewed student performance on the state tests, and examined the school's existing improvement plan. Yet, after all this emphasis on process issues and classroom observations, the eventual plan developed by the UCLA EET was short on substance. Their plan identified weaknesses at the school, but none of the intervention strategies recommended by the external evaluators mentioned the state academic content standards.

For example, the plan's first measurable objective to improve student academic performance states that "all [CVUHS] students will read at a level that allows them to be contributing members of society." Notice that this objective does not say students must read and perform at standards-based, grade-level proficiency. Thus it is possible to interpret the objective as allowing students to read at below grade level since such students could still be considered "contributing members of society." This vague language, and the loophole it creates, underscores the importance of linking improvement goals to the state standards, which inform teachers and principals as to the content knowledge their students must possess at each grade level.

In addition, the intervention strategy recommended to address low test scores at the school stated that: "the district will examine desegregated [sic, disaggregated] data, and the contributing factors within control of the school will be addressed through staff development on the teaching and learning process." The plan goes on to indicate that "ninth grade core teachers will develop criteria for the reading program, select the program and be trained pursuant to the program guidelines." Again, there is no mention of using the standards as learning guides or knowledge goals or their importance to any curriculum change.

Further, the Central Valley Union action plan slighted reforms based on empirical research in favor of much less rigorous strategies. One recommended step to improve student performance advised that "the school community will examine its beliefs of the learning process and develop a philosophy and models for classroom instruction." This New Age recommendation may have guaranteed harmony in the faculty lounge, but it did little to ensure that students received standards-aligned instruction. Also, the plan sought to downgrade the importance of state test results, despite the crucial importance of those results to the accountability process. Instead, it advocated different ways to assess student performance, including, among other things, student-led conferencing.

Much of the Central Valley Union action plan relied on subjective classroom observations. For instance, six out of the ten steps designed to improve student academic performance required classroom observation to evaluate the effectiveness of the action (see chart 1). The plan to motivate students required classroom observations, as did the vaguely described system of "student support."

It is telling that in steps 1 and 2—researching, designing, and implementing reading programs—those activities have no

Chart 1. Improving Student Performance

Measurable Objectives
- All [CVUHS] students will read at a level that allows them to be contributing members of society.
- Overall, all student groups will meet the required state-level growth mandates on the API. Students scoring in the 1st quintile will grow at twice the mandate and students scoring in the 2nd quintile will grow at 1.5 times the mandate.
- The district will provide a support system for all students.
- The district will utilize technology to enhance student learning and to improve the instructional support program.
- Staff development activities will support the objectives of this plan.

Supporting Action Steps

1. Research, design, and implement a Reading Intervention Program for 9th grade students. *Evaluation plan*: classroom observations and pre- and post-testing.

2. Research, design, and implement a Reading Program across the curriculum. *Evaluation plan*: classroom observations and collaborative review of student work.

3. The school community will examine its beliefs of the learning process and develop a philosophy and models for classroom instruction. *Evaluation plan*: articulated philosophy and models of classroom instruction, implementation of pedagogy based on the philosophy and models, and improved student performance on multiple measures.

4. The district will develop a system using multiple measures to assess student performance and inform teaching practices. *Evaluation plan*: student multiple measures data available to all teachers, classroom observations, and lesson plans.

5. Research, design, and implement a program that will develop skills and motivation for students to be successful in school. *Evaluation plan*: classroom observations and lesson plans.

6. Research, design, and implement a system of student support staff-wide. *Evaluation plan*: classroom observations, class scheduling, lesson plans, and student surveys and interviews.

7. Implement the Digital High School Grant. *No evaluation plan.*

8. Research methods to provide teachers timely access to student performance data. *Evaluation plan*: teacher surveys and interviews.

9. Develop technology as an instructional tool. *No evaluation plan.*

10. A committee will be formed to design and integrate staff development activities. *Evaluation plan*: staff development agendas, classroom observations, and student performance.[15]

discernible connection to the state standards, even though the state reading standards are perhaps the most important among all the standards. According to this plan it seems possible to design and put into operation a reading program that may be diametrically opposed to what is called for in the standards and the standards-aligned reading curriculum framework, which serves as the blueprint for implementing standards in the classroom.

Because the external evaluation process was not specifically linked to the state standards, the evaluations went wherever the biases of the evaluators took them. For instance, instead of laying the blame for poor student performance on the school's poor teaching methods or inadequate implementation of the state standards, the evaluators at CVUHS said that the low achievement of certain minority groups at the school was simply the result of socioeconomic status, higher transiency rates, lower parental education levels, and higher numbers of English-language learners. This evaluation shifted responsibility for poor student performance away from the school and also ignored the schools with similar demographics that have high student performance. Most knowledgeable observers viewed the pre-2004 II/USP evaluations and plans as highly unsatisfactory and unlikely to help schools meet their growth targets because the plans gave short shrift to student mastery of the subject matter content cataloged in the state standards.

Because many of the pre-2004 school improvement plans were not tied to improving standards-based instruction, the state board of education and the state superintendent of public instruction have created a substitute program for improving schools that fail to meet their growth targets under II/USP and the parallel High Priority Schools Grant Program. Under this substitute, the state superintendent of public instruction, with the approval of the state board of education, can designate a school assistance and intervention team for a school that fails to make significant growth in student achievement during its participation in the II/USP or the HPSGP.[16] What makes the new SAIT different from the pre-2004 external evaluation teams is that the SAIT is focused on ensuring that standards-aligned subject matter content is transmitted to students. The new SAIT approach concentrates on improving instruction using the standards as tools, guideposts, and objectives so students at those schools are able to achieve at grade level. But what remains troubling is the lack of current efforts to evaluate the success of SAIT officially.[17]

The new SAIT process, which is limited to reading/language arts and math, is based on designated "essential components" to improve classroom instruction and student academic performance. At the K–8 level, state documents describe nine components:

1. The school/district provides the most recent state board of education–adopted core instructional programs, including accelerated interventions for reading/language arts (2002-2008 adoption) and mathematics (2001-2007 adoption), documented to be in daily use in every classroom with materials for every student.
2. The school/district complies with and monitors implementation of required instructional time by grade level or programs, as specified in the state's curricular and instructional frameworks for reading/language arts and mathematics. This time should be given priority and be protected from interruptions.
3. The school/district has all principals and vice principals attend the appropriate school-level state-created Principal Training Program (forty hours of institute and forty hours of practicum) for the school/district's adopted reading/language arts and mathematics programs.
4. The district provides the school a substantial number of fully credentialed teachers in all grade levels, has a plan for staffing all classrooms with fully credentialed teachers; a substantial number of these teachers at all grade levels attend the state-created Mathematics and Reading Professional Development Program (forty hours of institute and eighty hours of practicum) for the district's adopted reading/language arts and intervention programs and mathematics program (which are taught in the classroom), and the district has a plan for training all remaining teachers.

5. The school/district implements a system for assessing, reporting, and monitoring student progress (using six- to eight-week curriculum-embedded assessments, which may include assessments available as part of the adopted program) and provides information to make instructional decisions based on the assessment data. These curriculum-embedded assessments are based on the adopted reading/language arts and the adopted mathematics programs. The purpose of these assessments is to provide timely data to teachers and principals to make decisions that will improve instruction and student achievement. In addition, they provide the basis for the monitoring system.

6. The school/district provides instructional assistance and support to teachers of reading/language arts and to teachers of mathematics. Some possible options include coaches/content experts who are knowledgeable about the adopted programs, who work inside the classroom to support teachers and deepen their knowledge about the content and the delivery of instruction; and specialists who have experience coaching teachers and who are knowledgeable about the adopted program.

7. The school/district facilitates and supports teachers' grade-level (K though six) or instructional program/department level (six through eight) collaboration in order to plan and discuss delivery (based on lesson study, with two one-hour monthly meetings recommended).

8. The school/district prepares and distributes an annual district/schoolwide pacing schedule for each grade-level (K through six) or instructional program/department level (six through eight) for both reading/language arts and mathematics (e.g., the annual plan, based on the school calendar, in order for all teachers to know when each lesson is expected to be taught and in what sequence to ensure content coverage).

9. The school/district general and categorical funds are used appropriately to support the reading/language arts and mathematics program goals in the school plan.

The nine components at the nine–twelve grade levels have a similar thrust:

1. The school/district provides state standards-aligned textbooks in all classrooms for all students enrolled in ninth- and tenth- grade English/language arts and mathematics courses (algebra 1 and remedial mathematics). State board of education–adopted intervention program texts are available for appropriate students.
2. The school's master schedule reflects effective use of instructional time and provides all students access to the English/language arts instruction needed to master the required skills to pass the language arts and writing components of the California High School Exit Exam (CAHSEE) and the necessary mathematics courses and instruction needed to master the required skills to pass the related component on the CAHSEE and in algebra 1.
3. The district provides the school's principal with state-created Principal Training Program and Leadership and Support of Student Instructional Programs through a state-authorized vendor. This requirement is substantially fulfilled when either the principal or the vice principal has successfully completed forty hours of the program focused on the adopted programs used at their site (reading intervention, algebra 1, and English/language arts), has completed the practicum, and a schedule is in place for other administrators to be trained within one year.
4. The district provides a substantial number of fully credentialed ninth- and tenth-grade English/language arts intervention teachers and algebra 1 and remedial mathematics teachers, and provides these teachers with professional development focused on state-adopted instructional materials for reading intervention, algebra 1, and adopted English/language arts and mathematics programs used at their site.
5. The school/district has an assessment and monitoring system (e.g., every six to eight weeks) to inform teachers and principals on student progress and effectiveness of

instruction in ninth- and tenth-grade English/language arts, algebra 1, and remedial mathematics classes. These assessments, usually referred to as curriculum embedded, should be based on the adopted English/language arts, algebra 1, and remedial mathematics textbooks, and can be the tests that are included in the adopted program. The purpose of these assessments is to help teachers and principals make decisions that will improve instruction and student achievement and provide a basis for the monitoring system.

6. The school/district provides instructional assistance and support to teachers of English/language arts, algebra 1, and remedial mathematics. Some possible options include coaches/content experts who are knowledgeable about the adopted programs, who work inside the classroom to support teachers and deepen their knowledge about the content and the delivery of instruction; and specialists who have experience coaching teachers and who are knowledgeable about the adopted program.

7. The school/district provides state board of education–approved intervention programs for all students working two or more grade levels behind in English/language arts and algebra 1 as assessed on the CAHSEE.

8. The school/district facilitates and supports teacher, department, and subject matter collaboration in order to plan and discuss lesson delivery, based on assessment data for the adopted programs in English/language arts and algebra 1.

9. The school/district general and categorical funds are used appropriately to support the reading/language arts and mathematics program goals in the school plan.

Because of these guiding components, the SAIT process avoids the rudderless nature of the pre-2004 II/USP external evaluations. The SAIT is designed to provide schools and districts with a consistent set of expectations, recommendations, and procedures designed to improve their ability to raise student achievement. Most important, the SAIT process is based on the principle that if students are to learn the subject matter described in the state's academic content standards, then schools must focus on teaching that subject-matter. The state's description of the SAIT process says:

> It is the intent of the SAIT process to help school implement these essential components by using the existing system for improving academic achievement including: (1) the California academic content standards embedded in the curricular and instructional frameworks, (2) the state board–adopted instructional programs (K–8) in reading/language arts and mathematics and standards-aligned instructional materials grades 9–12, and (3) the [state-created] teacher professional development programs and [state-created] principal training.

The California academic content standards are the core of the new SAIT process.

The SAIT process itself starts with schools and districts completing a self-assessment survey and collecting and reviewing the data on student achievement. The assistance team then makes a visit to the school to verify survey responses. During these initial stages, the assistance team determines which of the "essential components" are present or missing at the school. These initial activities, from assigning the assistance team to the schools and districts accepting the SAIT report and recommendations, must occur within ninety days of the assignment of the assistance team.

A Level I intervention takes place at schools that are missing some essential components; schools that have the components substantially in effect undergo a Level II intervention. Assistance teams will also recommend a Level II intervention if a school has gone through a Level I intervention and has all the essential components substantially in place but still fails after a full year to make significant growth in student achievement.

In 2003, the state board of education adopted criteria for SAIT providers. According to the board's requirements, SAIT providers must apply to review a specific grade span or spans, plus assure their expertise in the subject matter and instructional programs in use at the school. Further, the providers must deliver multilayered interventions, given the differing initial status and academic progress of schools. The board also requires that SAIT providers demonstrate recent success in working with low-performing schools through:

- Knowledge of state board–adopted academic content standards and frameworks
- Teaching standards-based reading, writing, language arts, and mathematics for students by grade span
- Knowledge and use of universal access materials and other strategies to help English learners acquire full academic proficiency in English and meet grade-level standards in the context of state statutory requirements
- Knowledge and use of state assessments, plus curriculum-embedded assessments, standardized, criterion-referenced, and other forms of assessments and their use to guide school planning
- Accelerated interventions for underperforming students and schools, including the state board–adopted reading intervention programs
- Professional development that addresses standards-based instruction focused on state board–adopted or standards-aligned instructional materials that are in use at the school
- Ability to provide the intensive support necessary for the school to successfully implement recommendations made by the SAIT.

On the basis of these various criteria and requirements, forty-five SAIT providers from both public and private entities were selected in 2003–2004. For instance, twenty-one county offices of education were selected as well as private consulting firms plus well-known specialist organizations such as the Reading Lions Center, which has gained fame for its successful educator training programs focused on phonics instruction.

The composition of the assistance team depends on the level of intervention. A Level I team includes educators who have experience at the appropriate level (e.g., elementary, middle, or high school), some of whom must have participated in either a principal training institute or a math or reading professional development institute. Level II team members include educators eligible for Level I teams, as well as content experts who have knowledge and experience with the state-approved reading and math programs used at the school. These content experts must understand the overall design of the math or reading program. They must be skilled enough to demonstrate effective methods for teaching the content, including the use of curriculum-embedded assessments. They must be able to show teachers how to make these math or reading materials accessible to all students and how to use the materials to accelerate the achievement of target populations of students. They must be able to show teachers how to plan and hold grade-level meetings in which they work collaboratively on improving teaching effectiveness.

For a Level I intervention, the assistance team assists in revising the school plan so that it includes the essential components. (As of now, there are no common guidelines in place for this all-important process of revising the plan.)[18] The assistance team works with the school to get the components in place and documents the fact that they are in use. Also, the assistance team works with the school and district liaison team to

- Establish benchmarks for student achievement
- Schedule monitoring visits by the assistance team (required at least three times a year)
- Identify areas of technical assistance
- Establish a schedule for periodic monitoring reports to the school, district, local board of education, and state.

The new SAIT approach brings the local district back in as a unit of change, supervision, and accountability. It aims to enhance the knowledge and capacity of the districts, for it is, after all, district officials who hire, fire, and control principals and teachers. Under the SAIT approach, the districts oversee the improvement efforts of the failing school on an ongoing basis. The SAIT plan also contains a school and district liaison team that must include the principal's district-level supervisor, the person who has the authority to fire that principal. The SAIT approach is managerially feasible, in part because it wisely minimizes the role of the state in operating the local school. The essential components provide minimal guidelines from the state and then let the schools and districts go to work within those guidelines.

One key difference between the pre-2004 II/USP external evaluations and the SAIT process is that the Level I SAIT process does not require subjective classroom observations. For example, if a school does not have enough standards-aligned textbooks, the assistance team will tell the district to purchase them. Thus the SAIT process identifies specific problems and recommends specific corrective actions and benchmarks for performance that leave little room for obfuscating.

The goal of a Level II intervention is thorough use of the essential components.[19] Level II intervention is more intensive and provides direct technical assistance, such as bringing in content experts or coaches in reading and math to work with teachers. The assistance team works with the school and district liaison team to write a revised school plan that focuses on improved, in-depth implementation of the essential components, in addition to the site work of the content experts and coaches, the monitoring and implementation of the plan, and the mandatory thrice-annual monitoring reports. The revised school plan must include:

1. The activities to be performed by the school and district liaison team
2. An activity time line for implementation, documentation, and monitoring
3. A system for reporting student achievement outcomes (every six to eight weeks) and identifying targeted staff to receive achievement reports
4. A process whereby content experts and coaches and the liaison team can meet regularly to discuss progress, modify the revised school plan, and address student achievement reports.

The new SAIT process never loses sight of the overall objective of improving student achievement. The pre-2004 II/USP external evaluations seemed to support process for the sake of process, ignoring the larger goal of improving student performance. Under the SAIT Level II intervention, the school plan must also detail how teachers and parents are to receive frequent assessment data that report on student academic progress. The plan may also address confirmed barriers or distractions that impede student achievement at the school.

The reports issued by the assistance team look nothing like the often nebulous documents issued by the pre-2004 II/USP external evaluation teams. The SAIT reports are clear and make precise, unambiguous recommendations. Objectives based on the nine essential elements are laid out; findings of minimal, partial, substantial, or full implementation are made; recommendations are provided; and initial actions required to implement the recommendation are listed. A school is not considered to have acceptably met its objectives unless the assistance team rates the school as having achieved all of its objectives, at least, at the level of "substantial implementation."

The SAIT Level I report for Seaview School (not its real name), located in an area on California's Central Coast, is in stark contrast to the evaluation of Central Valley Union High School discussed earlier. The Seaview report was filed after the assistance team reviewed the school and the district self-assessment survey for the presence of the essential components.[20] The assistance team developed a "gap analysis" that determined what evidence about performance was missing for each essential component. The assistance team met with teachers and the school and district liaison team to discuss discrepancies between the initial survey and the assistance team's assessments. The assistance team shared its findings for each component. For excerpts from the report that indicate the clarity of thought, presentation, and action, see chart 2.

The importance of each individual objective is apparent: The first objective (having standards-aligned textbooks) is critical; without them it is impossible to ensure that children are receiving standards-aligned instruction. A state-sanctioned independent evaluation of the high school exit exam found that classrooms using newer standards-aligned textbooks were far

Chart 2.

I. Instructional Program

Objective 1: The school/district provides the most recent state board of education–adopted core instructional programs, including accelerated interventions for reading/language arts (2002–8 adoption) and mathematics (2001–7 adoption), documented to be in daily use in every classroom with materials for every student.

Finding 1.1: Partially met. Some students have the most recent state board of education–approved instructional program materials in reading/language arts.

Recommendation: Purchase additional materials so that all students *on a daily basis* at all grade levels have and *appropriately use* the SBE–approved Houghton Mifflin *A Legacy of Literacy* (2003).

Initial Actions: (1) Each grade level will submit an initial list of needed student materials by Wednesday, January 14 to [the principal]. (2) Purchases will be made by February 10 for any missing student materials.

II. Instructional Time

Objective 2: The school/district complies with and monitors implementation of required instructional time by grade level or programs, as specified in the state's curricular and instructional frameworks for reading/language arts and mathematics. This time should be given priority and be protected from interruptions.

Finding 2.3: Substantially met. Seventy-five percent of the classroom teachers provided evidence that they are allocating the mandated instructional time for the adopted mathematics program.

Recommendation: Revise daily schedules to include appropriate time allocation by grade level for implementation of the adopted programs. Evidence must be provided that the time is given priority and protected from interruptions. The SAIT will work with the district/school liaison team to develop monitoring procedures.

Initial Actions: (1) All grade levels submitted schedules of time allocations in December 2003, revised to reflect specific time devoted to adopted materials, and resubmitted January 6, 2004. (2) Grade levels will immediately begin reallocating time to reflect revised schedules.

VI. Ongoing Instructional Assistance and Support for Teachers

Objective 6: The school/district provides instructional assistance and support to teachers of reading/language arts and to teachers of mathematics. Some possible options include coaches/content experts who are knowledgeable about the adopted programs, who work inside the classroom to support teachers and deepen their knowledge about the content and the delivery of instruction; and specialists who have experience coaching teachers and who are knowledgeable about the adopted program.

Finding 6.1: Minimally met. The school/district provides little or no instructional assistance to support teachers in delivering reading/language arts instruction using the adopted materials.

Recommendation: Develop and implement a plan to provide instructional assistance and support to teachers in reading/language arts.

Initial Actions: (1) Survey the teachers to determine the nature of instructional assistance needed. *(2)* The language arts SAIT lead will work with the District/School Liaison Team to provide additional instructional assistance support to teachers. *(3)* Hire a part-time recently retired teacher trained in the Houghton Mifflin materials to provide instructional assistance to the faculty. *(4)* Provide administrator services support to the principal so that she is able to focus on instructional leadership and support in the implementation of the adopted instructional materials during the school day.

VII. Lesson Pacing Schedule

Objective 8: The school/district prepares and distributes an annual district/schoolwide pacing schedule for each grade level (K–6) or instructional program/department level (6–8) for both reading/language arts and mathematics (e.g., the annual plan, based on the school calendar, in order for all teachers to know when each lesson is expected to be taught and in what sequence to ensure content coverage).

Finding 8.2: Minimally met. Inconsistent use of publisher-provided pacing schedules.

Recommendation: Develop, implement, and monitor a schoolwide plan to put in place an appropriate pacing schedule for the mathematics program in all grade levels to include English learner and special education student needs.

Initial Actions: (1) Weekly collaboration time will be used to develop, implement, and track pacing schedules. *(2)* The work in developing pacing schedules for Harcourt Brace provided by a neighboring district will be shared and implemented.[21]

more likely to cover the standards than classrooms using older, nonaligned textbooks.[22]

Also, the use of pacing plans in the eighth objective makes sense. If teachers are to cover the required content in full, they must allocate their time wisely. Critics of the pre-2004 school improvement approach contend that, in failing schools, teachers teach only "half the content."[23]

Further, the SAIT report contains no reference in its recommendations and initial actions to amorphous "classroom observations." Rather, the recommendations and initial actions pinpoint specific problems and precise solutions.

The Seaview report (see chart 2) is the first in a series of quarterly reports that will document the implementation of the essential components. The first report also creates a baseline for program components, including recommendations and initial actions.

The assistance team may serve schools like Seaview for a thirty-six-month period. If in that period the school makes significant growth for two consecutive years, it will exit the program. If the school fails to make significant growth, then the state superintendent can choose from several options, including closing the school.

So far, the reaction of schools to the SAIT interventions has been a combination of initial shock and subsequent, if grudging, support. The *Fresno Bee* newspaper, for example, reports that two low-performing schools in southeast Fresno were subjects of brutally honest evaluations by SAIT. The report for one school said that staff members did not "recognize or accept their professional responsibility for addressing student success and failure." The school's principal, however, admitted that the intervention resulted in an intensified schoolwide effort to align lessons with the state standards; increased teacher training on using new state-approved, standards-aligned textbooks; and involved closer monitoring by administrators to ensure that the standards are taught in the classroom. Teachers said that the interventions prompted staff members to make sure they had high expectations for all students and initiated a more systematic approach to teaching the standards. Finally, the interventions focused on using data from the standards-aligned state tests to determine student weaknesses. So far, state education officials have said they have been pleased with the progress and effort of the schools in implementing the SAIT recommendations.[24]

In addition to focusing on academic content and the state standards, the SAIT process accomplishes other important objectives. Whereas the state provides guidance, the SAIT process focuses on the district as a unit of change, supervision, and accountability.

The process enhances the capacity and knowledge of the districts, because they hire and fire personnel and control resources. The process is easier than the pre-2004 approach in the sense that it focuses on tools that are already available (i.e., the existing academic standards, standards-aligned textbooks, assessment devices in the textbooks, training and coaching directed toward using the textbooks, and state-created teacher and principal training programs.)

The new SAIT approach rests on the simple concept that if schools are successful in transmitting standards-based knowledge and skills to students, then student achievement will rise. Thus, what the SAIT approach does is bring standards-based coherence to remedial actions for failing schools. Principals, teachers, and district officials know what they have to do to improve because the same components and objectives are being used throughout California. They are constantly reminded of what they have to do because the same message of standards, curriculum-embedded assessments, and teacher training is repeated up and down the California educational system. The SAIT approach does not require impossibly large amounts of involvement by experts nor does it require principals who are supermen or superwomen. The SAIT approach provides guidelines that encourage educators currently working in the state's K–12 system to be more effective and productive.

California's experience provides a case study for the accountability expectations and school-intervention plans of the national NCLB law. By shining a light on this state's experience, we can see what the prospects are for fixing faltering public schools. All the California intervention programs (II/USP, HPSGP, and SAIT) have sought to take account of the NCLB requirements and satisfy them. On paper, each seems to meet the requirements. But it is an awkward, but telling, fact that two of the approaches did not work, even though they followed the law's procedures. The new SAIT approach is promising, but it may not work either. It deserves more careful monitoring than the cash-strapped state of California is giving it.

The American public school system is based on its local districts. California's SAIT system for fixing public schools relies on those districts to monitor improvement in their own schools.

California's experience shows that unfocused intervention pro-grams that have more to do with process than standards-ori-ented results are not likely to succeed. California also shows that a successful rescue program must include both a well-focused and sound research-based plan *and* a set of behavior-altering in-centives that the plan can actually be implemented as written. California has some carrots (in the form of school improvement funds), and NCLB has some sticks (like takeovers and restaffing). Time will tell if this is enough to concentrate the minds of California's educators.

Notes

The authors wish to acknowledge the research assistance of Kate Fein-stein and to thank Rae Belisle, Macke Raymond, Chester E. Finn Jr., John Chubb, Marion Joseph, and Alice Furry for comments on earlier drafts of the article.

1. By the Public Schools Accountability Act of 1999 at www.cde.ca.gov/ta/ac/pa/ (accessed May 3, 2004).

2. Such targeting is recommended by, for example, the Education Commission of the States. See *State Interventions in Low-Performing Schools and School Districts* (Denver, Colo.: Education Commission of the States, August 2002), 30.

3. New York's plan for failing schools (observation visits followed by an improvement plan) looks similar to California's pre-2004 ap-proach. See *State Interventions in Low-Performing Schools*, 14. But Cali-fornia's broad array of independent providers also resulted in widely different plans for improvement.

4. See http://sccac.lacoe.edu/new/dis.html (accessed April 30, 2004).

5. Jennifer O'Day and Catherine Bitter, "Evaluation Study of the Immediate Intervention/Underperforming Schools Program and the High Achieving/Improving Schools Program of the Public Schools Ac-countability Act of 1999," Final Report submitted to Evaluation Unit, Policy and Evaluation Division, California Department of Education, American Institutes for Research in partnership with Policy Analysis for California Education and EdSource, June 30, 2003, xi.

6. Ibid., xiii.

7. This problem is by no means unique to California. A review of school improvement efforts in Philadelphia found the same phenomenon. "The major findings from the assessment were that the schools were in desperate need of coherence. The School Improvement Plans were without focus and characterized by dozens of uncoordinated initiatives." See Nancy Streim and Jeanne Vissa, "Do Universities Have a Role in Managing Public Schools? Lessons from the Penn Partnership Initiative," *Penn GSE Perspectives on Urban Education*, 2, no. 2, no. 4 (fall 2003), at www.urbanedjournal.org/articles/articles/article0011.html.

8. All quotations in this paragraph come from April 2004 interviews by the authors with critics of the pre-2004 system.

9. On classroom observation as an integral part of teachers' professional development, see Morris L. Cogan, *Clinical Supervision* (Boston: Houghton Mifflin, 1972), 196.

10. Edward J. Morrison, "Performance Observation as an Approach to Teacher Evaluation," *Educational Horizons*, 52, no. 4 (summer 1974): 167–72. See also Carol T. Fitz-Gibbon and N. J. Stephenson, "Inspecting Her Majesty's Inspectors: Should Social Science and Social Policy Cohere?" paper presented at the European Conference on Educational Research, September 25–28, 1996; Howard N. Garb and Patricia Boyle, "Understanding Why Some Clinicians Use Pseudoscientific Methods: Findings from Research on Clinical Judgment," in Scott O. Lilienfeld, Steven Jay Lynn, and Jeffrey M. Lohr, eds., *Science and Pseudoscience in Clinical Psychology* (New York: Guilford Press, 2003), 17–38.

11. Streim and Vissa, "Do Universities Have a Role?"

12. Gunnar Handal and Per Lauvas, *Promoting Reflexive Teaching: Supervision in Practice* (Philadelphia: Society for Research into Higher Education; Milton Keynes, Eng.: Open University Press, 1987), ix–x, 50, as cited in Wendy Wang and Cathy Day, "Issues and Concerns about Classroom Observation: Teachers' Perspectives," paper presented at the annual meeting of the Teachers of English to Speakers of Other Languages, St. Louis, Mo., February 27–March 3, 2001) (ERIC Accession No. ED 467 734), 7.

13. "State Interventions in Low-Performing Schools," 22.

14. Julian R. Betts and Anne Dannenberg, "The Effects of Accountability in California," in Paul E. Peterson and Martin R. West, eds., *No Child Left Behind? The Politics and Practice of School Accountability* (Washington, D.C.: Brookings Institution, 2003), 208.

15. II/USP Action Plan for CVUHS, 1999.

16. The state board of education changed the name of the school improvement process from the previous designations of "academic audit"

or "scholastic audit" to "School Assistance and Intervention Team" (SAIT) in early 2003. Then in December 2003, the board changed the approach to be taken by the teams. For the sake of clarity, this chapter refers to the audit approach and the 2003 SAIT approach as the pre-2004 approach and refers to the SAIT approach after December 2003 as the new SAIT approach.

17. The authors acknowledge Macke Raymond for directing their attention to this point.

18. Ibid.

19. It will be somewhat difficult to evaluate how thorough schools have been in making use of the essential components. If one looks at the nature of components at the K through eight and nine through twelve levels, certain components lend themselves to quantitative measurement (number of textbooks, amount of teaching time, whether the textbooks are actually used and the extent to which teachers and principals make use of their training programs), but others do not. The authors wish to acknowledge the advice of Macke Raymond on this point.

20. For a newspaper account of a SAIT intervention in two Fresno schools, see Anne Dudley Ellis, "2 Schools Will Face Critical State Test: Fresno Students' Low Scores Led to Academic Audits," *Fresno Bee*, May 4, 2004, at www.fresnobee.com/local/story/8524242p-93707c.html (accessed May 4, 2004). The story stresses that the SAIT report was "scathing." It required alignment of lessons with state standards and increased teacher training on using state-approved textbooks. In general, it required the district to monitor and document school efforts.

21. "Seaview School" School Assistance and Intervention Team, "Findings Report #1," January 2004.

22. "Independent Evaluation of the California High-School Exit Exam (CAHSEE): AB 1609 Study Report—Volume 1," Human Resources Research Organization (prepared for the California Department of Education), Alexandria, Virginia, May 1, 2003), 48.

23. April 2004 interviews with the authors.

24. Ellis, "2 Schools Will Face Critical State Test."

7

A Conflict of Interest: District Regulation of School Choice and Supplemental Services

Paul E. Peterson

In January 2002, President George W. Bush signed into law No Child Left Behind (NCLB), a substantial revision of the Elementary and Secondary Education Act (ESEA), the compensatory education program initially enacted in 1965.[1] NCLB builds on prior ESEA legislation that had encouraged states to establish an accountability system. But, unlike the previous law, NCLB required states, if they wished to continue to receive federal funding, to set standards, develop and administer tests to see whether students reach those standards, and ensure that all students reach those standards within twelve years, reaching specific targets at various checkpoints along the way.

But what if schools fail to meet the specified targets? What are the consequences? Not many. For all the dire talk about the strictures NCLB places on states and localities, the negative consequences of failure are slight. In the first instance, schools are actually rewarded for failure: states have been asked to set aside about $230 million dollars of their NCLB dollars for the specific purpose of bringing failing schools up to standard.[2]

As for aversive therapy, there are but three treatments:

1. Schools are to be reconstituted if, after five years, they remain in need of improvement. (Because the provision has

141

not yet taken effect in more than a few places, this chapter does not assess its impact.)

2. Parents are to be given the choice of their child's attending another public school within their school district, if the child's school is found, for two years running, to be "in need of improvement" (in common parlance, a failing school). Although the provision takes effect only after a school fails to perform at the requisite level for two years in a row, its impact was felt the very school year NCLB was enacted (2001–2002, which we denote as Year 1) in states that had failing schools under previously established state standards.

3. Parents are to be given access to supplemental services funded by the federal government at levels ranging from $700 to $2,000 dollars, if their child's school is found to be failing three years in succession. Once again, this provision took effect in some districts in Year 1 because some schools had already been defined as failing under prior ESEA legislation.

Do these consequences give schools the needed incentives to improve the quality of their educational offerings so that no child will be left behind? If not, what needs to be done to strengthen the legislation so that its stated objectives can be achieved? A review of the evidence for the first three years of NCLB (Years 1, 2, and 3) reveals inadequate implementation, largely because of a basic conflict of interest at the local level. School districts are asked not only to operate the programs and services required by NCLB but also to ensure that their operations are in compliance with the law. If this arrangement were practiced in the banking industry, the Security and Exchange Commission would also be a brokerage firm.

Giving Students a Choice

During the first three years of NCLB's implementation, few students chose to leave failed schools—in large part because the law itself provided only limited choice options. Nonetheless, had the law been faithfully implemented by local school districts, many more families would have had access to alternative schools.

Legislative Provision

NCLB's pallid school choice provisions are politically understandable. At the time the law was passed, Congress was deeply divided over the amount of choice that should be provided parents as part of NCLB. On the one side, Republican leaders sought to carry out Bush's presidential campaign promise to give parents access to a private school if they were attending a public school that had failed three years running. On the other side, Senator Edward Kennedy and other leading Democrats insisted that inclusion of any school voucher provision would kill all hope for passage of school reform legislation. Partisan divisions ran deep and wide.

Congressional passage of the law required a bipartisan consensus, especially since Democrats had a majority in the Senate, and Republicans controlled the House of Representatives. Given this reality, White House officials backed away from the voucher promises made during the course of the campaign, to the dismay of key Republicans in the House of Representatives and their school choice supporters, who continued to insist that some form of choice be included in the final bill. Meanwhile, many Democrats and their public school interest-group allies were adamant that choice be minimized. Senator Kennedy, however, indicated that he would support a bill that had some limited forms of parental choice.[3]

The result was limited public school choice. Parents can choose any nonfailing schools within the district in which they reside. However, they do not have access to private schools under NCLB provisions. Nor do they have a choice of any charter school outside their district. Nor do parents have a choice of traditional public schools beyond the district line. Even within the district, the choice of another public school is limited. Parents with a child in an underperforming school cannot choose another underperforming one. In small districts with one school, all choice is precluded. In big cities, with many schools designated as in need of improvement, the choice is very limited.

Administrative features of the choice provisions are no less restrictive. School districts, the very entities that have resisted choice in the past, are responsible for administering those provisions. Thus if few parents are exercising choice under NCLB, it is not so much because parents are uninterested in an alternative educational setting as that administration of this provision of NCLB is assigned to the same entity—the school district—that is operating schools designated as failing. It's a bit like putting prisoners in charge of the jail.

The Numbers

A school must be designated as failing for two consecutive years before the choice provisions take effect. But because many schools had been designated as failing under previous state accountability systems, millions of parents had this option as early as Year 1 (2001–2002). By Years 2 and 3 (school years 2002–2003 and 2003–2004, respectively), the option had spread to millions more.

Despite the apparent availability of the choice option to millions of parents, I estimate that, as of Year 2, about only 1 percent of the eligible population took advantage of the choice provisions. The percentage increased somewhat in Year 3, but the U. S. Department of Education admits that it remains around 1 percent. That estimate is confirmed by newspaper reports, statistics provided by some school systems and state departments of education, and a few independent studies.

Initial newspaper accounts generally reported only tiny numbers of transfers under the school choice provisions in Year 1 of NCLB. In New York City, just 1,507 out of 220,000 eligible students transferred. In Chicago, it was just 800 out of 125,000 young people. Los Angeles had less than 50 participating students from among 200,000 eligible.[4] Nor was it just the big cities that were having trouble implementing this provision of the law. In the summer of 2002, there were fewer than 500 transfers in Atlanta, and just 331 in Fulton County, Georgia.[5] The number in Howard County, Maryland, was forty-three.[6] In Worcester, Massachusetts, just 1 of 4,689 eligible students had transferred by the end of Year 1.[7]

By Year 2, Howard County's numbers had expanded by another thirty-nine students, roughly doubling the initial number. But in all of Maryland, as of June 2003, only 709 transfers seem to have occurred. Virginia had 226 transfers, while the District of Columbia had just 148 students moving from one school to another. The same pattern existed elsewhere. In Chicago, only 529 had actually taken seats at a new school as the Year 2 school year was beginning.[8]

These numbers, taken mainly from newspaper accounts, are scattered and not altogether comparable. But Michael Casserly, executive director of the Great City Schools Council, obtained similar results after gathering information directly from offices of forty-six of the nation's largest school districts (hereinafter referred to as the big-city districts).[9] He estimated that in Year 1 of NCLB just 5,660 students in all forty-six of the big-city districts transferred from one school to another under the provisions of the law. In Year 2, 17,878 students transferred, three times the number in Year 1, but still less than 0.3 percent of the 6.8 million students enrolled in these districts. If one were to assume that these forty-six districts are representative of the nation as a whole, approximately 170,000 students nationwide in Year 2 were exercising choice under NCLB.

This overestimates the national pattern, however. Big-city school districts have a higher percentage of failing schools than do suburban and rural districts. They also have more schools within their district to which students might move. And Casserly's data came from districts that responded to his inquiry, presumably the administratively more coherent of the big-city districts. Adjusting for these factors, the number of students exercising choice was most likely only half this figure, well below 100,000—less than 0.2 percent of the nation's more than 50 million public school students.

Of course, many students were not transferring because they were not attending a failed school—and thus not eligible for transfer under the law. Only about 20 percent of the students in these big-city districts attended failing schools. These 1,694 failing schools had 1,168,659 students. Of all these students eligible for transfer under the provisions of the law, 17,878 students transferred in Year 2 of NCLB—about 11 students per school, or about 1.5 percent of those eligible. That may be taken as a high-end estimate of the national transfer rate. Adjusting downward, it is probable that less than 1 percent of students in schools designated as failing transferred to another school. A Washington think tank, the Center on Education Policy (CEP), also estimated that the participation rate in Year 2 was 1 percent.[10]

According to CEP, participation rates increased to 2 percent in Year 3.[11] In San Diego, the participation rate in Year 3 was as high as 2 percent of the 75,000 students deemed eligible.[12] (A similar 2 percent transfer rate was also reported for a suburban county in Maryland.)[13] However, the CEP estimate, though similar to those in Maryland and San Diego, probably exaggerates the nationwide participation rate. For one thing, it is based on school district survey data provided before the release of a full list of schools and students eligible for participation (reducing the size of the denominator for the estimate). Also, CEP's own case study data reveal only a 0.5 percent participation rate in Year 3 in those school districts where data were gathered in a more precise manner. Other anecdotal sources of information also reveal low participation rates in Year 3. Dekalb County, Georgia, reported an uptick of participating students from a tiny 28 students to just 183 students,[14] and, in Columbus, Ohio, transfers hardly budged—from 530 to 545 students.[15] In Chicago, only 737 students remained in a transferred school throughout Year 3, and the projection of available seats for Year 4 was a paltry 547.[16] New York allowed more than seven thousand of its more than one million students to transfer in Year 3, but planned to cut the number to around a thousand in Year 4.[17] Meanwhile, in Cleveland, only thirty-five transfers were reported for Year 3.[18]

Such evidence suggests a high degree of variability among districts. A little more than half the eligible schools in urban districts were offering choice, whereas only about a quarter of the districts in rural areas were doing so.[19]

Choice Benefits

It is too early to tell whether choice under NCLB benefits the students who exercise it, or what impact their departure has had on the schools they have left. To the best of our knowledge, only one study has attempted to estimate the impact of NCLB choice on student performance. The Chicago school district reported that the test scores of students who transferred indicated that they were learning at a higher rate in both reading and math at their new school than the rate at which they had been learning at their previous, failing school. And there was no sign of harm to either sending or receiving schools.[20] Although the gains were large, the number of observations was small. Whether these initial results will be found again in Chicago and repeated elsewhere remains to be seen.

Transfer Requests

The number of students requesting transfer under NCLB was considerably higher than those who actually moved. In Year 2 the number of requests for transfer in the big-city districts totaled 44,372 students, still only about 2.5 percent of all those eligible for transfer. In that year, New York City sent out 300,000 letters notifying parents of the transfer opportunity but received requests from only 8,000 parents, a less than 3 percent response rate. Chicago's response rate was higher (7 percent), but Cleveland's was only 0.3 percent and San Diego's 0.1 percent.[21] The number of transfer requests appears to have climbed in Year 3, doubling in Columbus, Ohio, for example.[22] Nonetheless, requests came from only a small percentage of the eligible population.

Are Parents Satisfied—or Not Well Informed?

The paucity of transfer requests might indicate high levels of parental satisfaction with their child's school, even if it were designated as failing. Nationwide, most parents express satisfaction with the school their child attends, and most would not exercise choice, even if readily available.[23] Nonetheless, a substantial percentage of parents are unhappy with their low performing schools. According to a ten-city Massachusetts survey conducted by Harvard scholar William Howell, nearly 30 percent of parents in failing schools give their school a low grade (C, D, or F); only 15 percent of parents in schools that met NCLB standards gave a similarly low grade.[24] Clearly, a sizable number of parents are concerned about the quality of their failing schools.

Many parents also seem prepared to leave their failing schools. When the Massachusetts parents of children in failing schools were asked a series of questions about their schools, they indicated they would prefer another school. When asked if they preferred a private school to their own school, 45 percent said yes. When asked whether there was another public school in their district preferable to their own, 23 percent said yes. Asked whether a school in another district, 18 percent said yes. And 18 percent said yes when asked if they preferred a charter school. In short, there appears to be considerable pent-up demand for greater choice.[25]

This demand does not translate into actual requests for a transfer because many parents have not been notified about the choices that are available. In the ten Massachusetts cities, only 30 percent of the parents with a child attending a failing school correctly identified its status; in Buffalo, New York, only 25 percent of eligible families knew of their right to transfer their children.[26] The percent correctly identifying a school's status was lower for those families (1) whose children qualified for a free lunch; (2) where the mother was no more than a high school graduate; (3) if the child was living in a single-parent family, or (4) if the child came from a family where the mother was foreign born. Parents were more likely to identify the school's status correctly if the parent was a volunteer at the school, a member of the PTA, or had a family member who worked in a local public school.[27]

Still, a lack of information, especially by disadvantaged parents, is to be expected when a choice program is in its infancy. It takes time for parents to learn about the options, to consider whether the alternative is superior to their child's current situation, and to calculate the costs of making a change. Even aggressive choice programs initially recruit no more than about 5 percent of those eligible to participate.[28]

Over time, the number of participants gradually increases, however. In Milwaukee, where a wide range of school choice has been in place for nearly a decade, about 30 percent of the students are exercising choice: 15 percent use a voucher, and the other 15 percent attend charter schools. Perhaps the percentage of choice participants under NCLB will gradually increase, reaching the level attained in Milwaukee, once the program has been in effect for a sustained period of time. This expectation seems reasonable, given the percentage of parents who, when surveyed, express an interest in exercising choice.

But a closer look at the obstacles to school choice preclude such a rosy scenario. The choice provisions of the law are self-limiting, and school districts are doing little to foster school choice. Unless the choice provisions are loosened and administration of the program is placed under an independent agency not controlled by local school districts, it is unlikely that NCLB will become a major vehicle for the exercise of school choice.

Receiving School Eligibility

Parents have a choice of school within their school district, provided that a receiving school is not itself failing. The number of schools designated as failing is climbing steadily, as the standard set by NCLB rises with each passing year. In New York City, for example, the number of failing schools in Year 4 increased by another 43 schools to a total of 497—more than 40 percent of the city's schools.[29] As a result, the number of eligible receiving schools is dwindling in many big-city school districts, limiting the number of available receiving schools. As the remaining receiving schools become increasingly crowded, there is little choice left.

The amount of school choice provided under NCLB thus needs to be expanded to include schools outside the district; all charter schools, wherever located; and all schools within the district, regardless of whether or not a school is designated as failing. After all, not all schools designated as in need of improvement are identical. And a school can be effective for a particular child, even if it does not fulfill all the NCLB requirements.

Practical Limitations on School Choice

Some of the constraints under which the choice program now labors are understandable, can be easily corrected, and may well be fixed by making modest adjustments to NCLB.[30] Schools become eligible for participation in the choice program only after test results show that they are in need of improvement. Often, these test results are not available until well into the summer or the fall of the next school year, too late for districts, schools, and parents to respond. If choice is to be provided under these circumstances, district administrators must disseminate information under tight time constraints, parents must make hasty decisions, children may need to be transferred within the middle of the year, school district administrators must quickly concoct new transportation plans, and individual schools may have to adjust staffing in response to changes in enrollment.

The seriousness of these problems is evident from reports from big-city school administrators. Of those who responded to the Casserly survey, fourteen districts reported that they did not notify parents of the choice option until after the school year began, another seven districts notified parents in August, and eleven districts did so in June or July.[31] When notified that late, San Diego parents were simply unwilling to consider a new school, partly because "students had already started their academic year at their local school before learning of their busing options."[32] It was difficult for the school district to respond more quickly, given the tasks that needed to be performed:

> Once the list of new [failing] schools is released to the district, the bus routes must be overhauled on short notice. This is extremely time consuming because a fixed number of buses must somehow be stretched to meet the new NCLB choice requirements while continuing to serve the [students already enrolled in choice programs].

Transportation is just one of the issues. Even communicating with parents in a legally appropriate manner creates a challenge. According to one San Diego administrator,

> This year we mailed out 105,000 letters overall to parents. . . . For each letter, a draft must be reviewed by [the] Legal [department], [the] Communications [department], and the departments that deal with teachers, supplemental services, and busing. Then we need to print and deliver all of these letters just at the time when our business services department is already fully booked [with other items that are distributed at the beginning of the school year]. So we have to put the contract out to bid and wait the required number of days before choosing a contractor.[33]

Because of such practical problems, parents often find about a choice opportunity too late to make use of it, and school districts, even if willing to assist in the choice process, incur substantial administrative costs. Such problems could be corrected by simply making the choice option available for the subsequent year—and by keeping the choice program in place until a school has proven itself not to be in need of improvement for three years running.

Discouraging Participation in the Choice Program

If practical problems were the only concern, they could be fixed with a minimum of legislative and administrative tinkering.

More serious are the signs that many districts are actively discouraging school choice. According to one survey, only half the schools eligible to offer parents a choice are actually doing so.[34]

Informing Parents

For one thing, many parents report that they have received little information about NCLB from their school district. Although 69 percent of parents attending schools in ten urban districts in Massachusetts say they have heard of NCLB, and 52 percent say they know about its choice provisions, only 24 percent said they had obtained their information from the school district. The general news media, not the school district, were said to be the most important source of information.[35]

Incentives

School districts may be reluctant to provide extensive information about choice provisions, because schools that are potential recipients of choice students are often reluctant to accept them. NCLB requires that transfers be given first to low-performing students, so receiving schools tend to look askance at new arrivals. They worry that the NCLB students will be stigmatized by faculty and students. In San Diego, one receiving school principal observed: "We aren't *afraid* that our schools will fail—we *know* they will."[36]

Meanwhile, sending schools fear their best students will leave. Claims one San Diego administrator, "Our prediction we have is that all [failing] schools' test scores will fall because better students appear to be leaving [failing] schools."[37] The complaints of the receiving and sending schools are not necessarily contradictory. A good student at a failing school may not appear that strong to administrators at a top-performing receiving school.

Limited Options

Because of opposition from both sending and receiving schools, districts are limiting the choices available to parents. On average, big-city districts gave parents just two or three options. A couple of districts provide only one, though federal regulations require at least two.[38] The practice seems more widespread in more than just big-city districts. When William Howell interviewed an administrator in Worcester, Massachusetts, as part of his study of implementation in that city, the administrator explained, "The feds told us we had to offer a choice, not the parents' choice, but a choice."[39]

Discouraging Transfers

Not only are choices limited, but district officials often deliberately discourage parents from considering a transfer. As Howell points out:

> [Public] schools have every incentive to present [NCLB] as muddled and misinformed, to highlight new and innovative programs being initiated within the public school system, and to make the process of switching schools . . . as cumbersome as possible.[40]

In the letter sent to parents, the Worcester district explained that "in need of improvement" did not mean the school was failing but only that "although these schools are succeeding in some areas, there is still room for growth." The letter then examines the deficiencies of NCLB definitions and measurements. After sharply criticizing the law under which the district is operating, the letter describes various problems associated with transferring to another school, including, "In most instances, because of space limitations [a problematic basis for refusing choice (see discussion below)], we may not be able to transfer every child in a family to the same school." And, the letter concludes, the child's current school is making major strides forward: "We believe that your child's school is on its way towards achieving the NCLB goals. The principal and teachers at your child's school have implemented new programs and services during the school day as well as after school."

If, after pondering this letter, parents still wish to transfer, they must first meet with the principal, who explains why the child's current placement should be accepted as satisfactory. If the parents persist, they must meet with the staff of the Parent Information Center, who often tell parents that the parents' choice of school is not available. It is hardly surprising that only one Worcester student succeeded in running this gauntlet and transferring to another school.[41]

The experience of Lauren LaCroix, a parent in Clarkston, Georgia, was not dissimilar to the one that took place in Worcester. It took her months to persuade school officials to make the transfer she desired. "I just wonder if more people would have done it if it was made easier for them," she said. "Ultimately, it makes them [school officials] look bad that the . . . people are wanting to transfer out."[42]

Student Eligibility

Some school administrators are so resistant to providing choice to parents that they have seized on a loophole in the law that gives choice only to those who are "enrolled" in a failing school. Interpreted narrowly, the law does not require choice for newcomers to a school or a student in an entry-grade cohort, who must spend a year in a failing school before applying for transfer. In Howard County, Maryland, for example, the school system denied a parental request for transfer on these grounds.[43]

Overcrowding

Yet it is the overcrowded school issue that has become the focal point of local resistance. Whether or not a school is overcrowded is often a judgment call. Schools can add students by including more students in a class, by placing classes in rooms previously set aside for special service activities, or by adding portable classrooms. No principal likes to take these steps, but hundreds are asked to do so every year, as the number of students in a vicinity fluctuates from one year to the next.

Still, the overcrowded school is thus the easiest and best excuse for denying a family access to the school of their choice. From the very beginning, many districts denied transfers on just these grounds. No less than 73 percent of the states reported that the school choice question raised capacity issues.[44] Recognizing how easy it would be for schools to be declared "overcrowded," the U. S. Department of Education issued a guideline saying that limited capacity was not an appropriate grounds for refusing students choice under NCLB.[45] Nonetheless, as the Worcester example suggests, some school districts seem to be denying transfers for this reason. One San Diego administrator's complaints reveal how deeply the resistance is embedded: "In theory, if we have 1,000 kids at a [failing] school and they all want to leave, we have to move them to [nonfailing] schools. Nobody knows how to limit a school designed for 200 students from expanding to 1,200."[46]

The topic also came up in an online chat between the U. S. secretary of education Rod Paige and New York City school officials. Local officials asked Paige what they should do when requests were made to schools that were oversubscribed. The secretary responded by saying,

> The school district can come up with innovative ways to meet the students' needs. They can use supplemental services sooner, can create charter schools, and can create schools inside of schools. They can even use technology to provide more options to parents. All of these choices can be accomplished by effectively utilizing Title I funds. The bottom line is these students need extra assistance to attain the education they deserve.

Nowhere does the secretary explicitly waive the federal mandate to transfer if a school is oversubscribed. Yet local school officials interpreted these comments as saying that students did not need to be transferred to oversubscribed schools, as federal guidelines instructed. In the words of one New York City official: "Some of the factors that are under consideration are the capacities of the schools which would receive transfers, the disruptive nature of transfers during the middle of the school year, and the ability to provide appropriate choices to students and their families. . . . We are very concerned about the disruptive nature of transfers on a school system where there may be limited capacity to absorb more transfers in midyear."[47]

The issue remained pressing in New York City as late as the summer of 2004, when the district indicated it was planning to cut the number of students who would be allowed to transfer from around seven thousand students in Year 3 to around a thousand in Year 4. Overcrowding of schools was offered as the justification for this sharp step backward. "We are trying to be sure that there really are available seats when we offer a transfer," said one district official. Similarly, in Chicago, no high school transfers are being allowed in Year 4, because of the lack of available seats in better performing high schools.[48]

Yet there were signs that factors other than crowding were important to the decision-making process. In the words of the president of the principals' union: "Principals are held accountable for students' scores, but they haven't had these children long enough to really make an impact." And other officials complained that transportation costs had run as high as $20 million in Year 3. Seeming to acquiesce in the decision made in New York, a federal official said that NCLB did not require a transfer if overcrowded conditions created safety problems for students.[49]

The Department of Education says that, under NCLB, it cannot allow districts to forestall choice simply because a potential receiving school is overcrowded. At the same time, it will not insist on transfers, if safety is jeopardized as a result of the influx of students. These are decisions that must be made on the ground. Unfortunately, those making the judgments often appear to be reluctant to give parents the choice they request.

Summary and Recommendations

There is reason to believe that, in the short run, about 5 percent of families, and, in the longer run, somewhere between 15 and 30 percent of parents in failing schools, may be interested in transferring to another school, if given a clear opportunity to do so. That has not happened. The actual transfer rate from one public school to another within the same district among eligible families appears to be less than 1 percent.

The low transfer rate can be partly attributed to practical difficulties of implementing the legislation, difficulties that may be better managed with the passage of time. Transportation problems are challenging until routines can be developed. Finding ways of communicating effectively with parents is not easy. The designation of schools as failing just before the beginning of the school year prevents both school officials and parents from planning a child's education in an orderly manner.

But there are strong signs that local school officials are both openly and passively resisting NCLB choice provisions. They have good reasons for doing so. Both sending and receiving schools appear opposed to school choice, the first because it does not want to appear to be failing, the second because it fears the needy students who are transferring. District administrators dislike the logistic problems involved in making the transfer.

As a result, school districts make only minimal efforts to comply with NCLB law and regulations. They notify parents when it may be too late to make a convenient transfer. Parents who inquire about the possibility of a transfer are discouraged from pursuing the matter. The choices offered to them are often limited, sometimes to a degree that violates federal guidelines.

If the choice provisions of NCLB are to become more effective, the following steps need to be taken:

1. Establish a nonprofit or for-profit organization separate from the school system that has the responsibility for communicating with parents about their rights and opportunities under NCLB choice provisions. That entity

should have the responsibility for facilitating requested transfers and identifying whether receiving schools are too crowded to accept transfers.

The new entity should also take special steps to (a) communicate with families whose native language is not English; (b) help arrange transportation services, making sure they are available indefinitely to any student exercising choice under NCLB provisions; (c) ensure that all students assigned to failing schools are eligible for choice, regardless of whether they have actually been in attendance at that school; and (d) facilitate a family's preference to keep all their children in the same school.

2. Broaden the range of choice to include schools in other districts, charter schools regardless of their location, and private schools, religious or secular.

3. Provide parents a choice among all schools within a district, whether or not they are officially designated as failing. The failing designation obscures a range of school performances, and not all schools designated as failing are inappropriate for a particular child.

Tutoring and Other Supplemental Services

Currently, public schools provide educational services for only a limited portion of the day. Despite the increasing need for a well-educated population, and despite the growing number of families in which no adult is in the home during the workday, the amount of time in public school has actually declined both over the past half century in the number of days of the year and the number of hours of the day.[50] Meanwhile, in a number of countries that score particularly high on international examinations (Japan, Korea, Singapore, and Taiwan), many students attend privately administered after-school programs. NCLB's supplemental services (in common parlance, free tutoring) are a beginning toward the creation of a similar set of institutions in the United States.

If a school has been designated as failing for three years running, parents are eligible to apply for free tutoring for their child, by either the school district or another provider. Because some states had preexisting accountability systems, under which schools were immediately designated as failing, the free tutoring provision came into play as early as Year 1.

As in the case of the school choice provisions, the free-tutoring provision of NCLB was initially a compromise between those committed to school vouchers and those strongly opposed to them.

As a compromise, the provision is ambiguous, inconsistent, and confusing. Most disturbing, it assigns to the school district primary responsibility for the provision's administration—even though districts may offer the services that other entities seek to provide. These supplemental services, moreover, are paid for by federal funds that districts may use for other purposes if the demand for tutoring is small. In other words, the more tutoring supplied, the less money districts have for their regular school budget. In part because of this conflict of interest, the percentage of students receiving supplemental services in the early years of the program remained limited. In addition, there is a danger that in the long run the program will not benefit from the full power of the competitive market.

The Law and Regulations

As mentioned, parents of students at schools that have failed for three years may choose a provider to supply free tutoring or some other form of supplemental educational service for their children. Twenty percent of the funds going to the district under Part A of NCLB may be used for this services, if parents so request; that amount could be as much as $2.4 billion.[51] The cost of the services may range from $700 to $2,000 per pupil, depending on the locality. Significantly, the school district may use these funds for its own purposes if parental demand does not consume the entire amount. To become a provider, a profit or non-profit entity must be approved by the state department of education. Providers sign contracts with school districts, even though the districts themselves may have been approved by the state as a provider of those same services.

The Numbers

The Department of Education has yet to issue an official count of either the number of students eligible to receive services or the number of students actually receiving them. But a private provider of supplemental services, Sylvan Education Solutions, estimates that enough funds are available to serve 1.5 million children. It estimates that in Year 1 only an estimated 30,000 to 40,000 children took advantage of the opportunity.[52] But by Year 2, in big-city school districts alone, a total of 113, 707 students in 1,196 schools were receiving free tutoring services under NCLB—112 students per school, a much larger number than the average number of students (eleven) per school exercising choice in these big-city districts.[53]

Although reports are scattered for Year 3, the information available indicates that the program has expanded. According to the California state department of education, 4 percent of eligible students are taking advantage of the opportunity.[54] Elsewhere, the take-up rate seems considerably higher. In both Louisville, Kentucky, and New York City, some 12.5 percent of the eligible students were participating in the tutoring program.[55] Virginia's state department reported that about 11 percent of its eligible students were receiving tutoring services.[56] In Milwaukee the percentage was as high as 20 percent.[57]

In other words, it appears that the free-tutoring provision of the law is being implemented much more rapidly than the school-choice provision. As of Year 3, I estimate the take-up rate among eligible students to be around 5 percent. The precise percentage is difficult to estimate because participation rates vary greatly from one district to another, depending on how aggressively tutoring is being promoted by school districts and private providers. My estimate is much smaller than the one provided by the Center on Education Policy, which asked district administrators to estimate the number of students receiving supplemental services. Although this survey yielded other useful information, these particular results seem highly problematic. For one thing, they report that the percentage of students actually receiving services declined from 46 percent in Year 2 to 25 percent in Year 3, suggesting a trend away from the use of tutoring services, when all other sources indicate otherwise.[58] Those district officials who filled out the questionnaire very likely misunderstood this question

Growth in participation rates can be expected to gain further steam in the next few years. For one thing, many more schools will be identified as failing for three years running. More important, a strong set of interests are rapidly forming around the free tutoring provision, interests that are likely to pressure school districts into more effective implementation of the legislation. More than one thousand free-tutoring providers—large and small, religious and secular, for-profit and nonprofit—are listed by the states. Some of these are well-established providers of tutoring services, namely, Kaplan K–12 Learning Services, Kumon Math and Reading Centers, Sylvan Education Solutions, Hunting Learning Center, and Princeton Review.[59] These providers will likely form a coalition in an attempt to influence the future development of policy.

But some—perhaps many—states and school districts can be expected to try to check this growth, and they have tools that allow them to do so. And there are numerous administrative problems impeding program expansion. It remains to be seen whether these administrative problems are temporary difficulties that a program experiences at its early stages or whether they are harbingers of more concerted public school resistance to the entry of new organizations providing education services. It is too early to draw firm conclusions, but it is worth considering the multiple factors currently inhibiting effective implementation of the free tutoring provision.

Benefits from Supplemental Services

There is as yet no systematic information on the benefits to students of participating in the tutoring program. Unfortunately, the law does not require the systematic collection of information on the test performance of students who are being tutored on state accountability examinations. As the tutoring program becomes increasingly well established, it is important that information on student performance be obtained. Such information should be collected by the provider, so that parents, when making a choice, can be informed about the effectiveness of various tutoring programs.

Factors Limiting Access to Tutoring Programs

The number of participants in tutoring programs, though climbing more rapidly than the numbers participating in school choice, remains a small fraction of all those eligible. A wide variety of factors are limiting participation rates, ranging from a lack of interest among eligible families to a lack of incentives to promote these services by school districts.

Parental interest

Many school districts report a lack of parental interest in and knowledge about the tutoring program. As one program administrator in Portsmouth, Virginia, observed: "We have not had the parent response that perhaps we anticipated. I think part of it is it's new. They're just unfamiliar with it."[60] More systematic information about parental interest in after-school programs has yet to be collected. Once parents are well informed, the level of interest in an after-school tutoring program could be substantial, especially since the demand for after-school programs by working couples is rapidly growing.

Adverse financial incentives

If parents are to become well informed about tutoring programs, school districts will need to employ aggressive recruitment programs. Practical problems interfere, however. Schools are not identified as failing until the summer or well into the new school year in which tutoring services are to be made available. Districts must then organize their own tutoring programs or sign contracts with providers and then inform parents of services being offered, all of which creates a long delay between eligibility and the service being provided.

But the practical problems can be addressed, if the districts have strong incentives to do so. Unfortunately, financial incentives—and political pressures—operate in opposite directions. If requests fall short of monies available under Part A, the school district may use funds for other purposes. When asked for ways of improving NCLB, one administrator said, quite frankly, "Eliminate the Supplemental Services provision; it is very expensive and is of minimal value."[61] Union leaders are no less skeptical. In New York, for example, the spokesperson for the New York State United Teachers, the state's largest teachers union, said, "Our concern is that it is going to be difficult if not impossible to track whether or not this money is being spent effectively."[62]

Given such pressures, districts may be tempted to provide limited information to parents about the free tutoring program, especially if the money is to go to an outside provider. According to a California state department of education report, 71 percent of the districts in which students were eligible for services did not have a tutoring program in place, saying that parents had "declined the service."[63] But a study by the Center on Education Policy reports that "parents thought the letters informing them about services were too long and complicated and buried key information."[64] This would be less of a problem were school districts to allow private providers to contact parents directly about the tutoring option. Because these providers have a stake in a large enrollment—and the school district does not—one could anticipate that they would employ a more aggressive recruitment strategy.

Conflict of interest

Not only do school districts provide the main point of contact with parents, but they themselves provide free tutoring and other supplemental services, thereby creating a conflict of interest between their role as provider and arbitrator among alternative providers. In fact a quarter of all providers currently approved are public entities, such as school districts or similar entities.[65] For example, the after-school program of the Worcester public schools received certification from the state. Because the district was a provider, private providers were deterred from seeking a contract with the district. As an administrator of one well-known provider explains, "The school district is the owner of the relationship between provider and the parent. And I can't get in." Even when a company is able to secure a contract with a district, it does not have access to the names of families eligible for tutoring. Instead, it must rely on referrals from the district. But if the district is running its own program, "it's like asking a BMW dealer to extol the benefits of buying a Volvo."[66]

When given anonymity, school administrators state frankly their suspicion of private providers. In one survey, the following comments were collected:

> Districts should be able to use the funds to provide their own programs using their best teachers.
> Supplemental Service funds should go to districts that would provide services without the profit motive.
> I would not use federal funds to support a program being operated by individuals not held to the same standards that public school employees are held to.
> Supplemental Services for any qualified provider will cause a cottage industry to develop that will be driven by profit and not academics.[67]

Given such suspicion of private providers, school districts may look for legal constraints that can be interpreted as requiring that they retain control of tutoring programs. Such legal hooks are not hard to find. For instance, the law says that the provider must "ensure that instruction provided and content used . . . are consistent with the instruction provided and content used by the local educational agency and State, and are aligned with State student academic achievement standards."[68]

This is being interpreted as saying that school systems themselves should provide tutoring services because they are best able to ensure that services are properly "aligned." In the words of a San Diego administrator:

> We're an ideal provider because we can provide this as part of a coherent system. The district already has in place a set of pre-

ventive measures and interventions for students who lag behind. A student can now spend another 90 minutes with her same teacher who knows what she needs. Coherence is everything.[69]

Coherence theory provides the San Diego school district with a justification for becoming the largest provider for its own students. The theory is likely to spread. In Milwaukee, for example, about three-quarters of all tutoring is provided by the school district itself.[70]

Certification of providers

The number of private providers is unnecessarily limited in many states, some of whom "set deadlines for [receipt of] their applications in very short, and seemingly arbitrary, windows of time." And states can judge applications severely. Colorado has "almost two dozen measures by which an applicant's quality is judged, including the program's record of effectiveness and its plan to monitor future performance." Because of the wide range of state administrative practice, reporter Siobhan Gorman tells us, the number of providers in a state is unrelated to the number of students eligible for services.[71]

States have approved only a small number of faith-based organizations as providers. Although religiously affiliated schools serve approximately 10 percent of the population, they are so far only 3 percent of all providers certified to offer free tutoring services.[72] It is not known whether this low participation rate is due to a lack of applications by providers or discrimination against faith-based institutions by state departments of education.

An oligopolistic market

The law provides no clear guidelines as to the number of providers with which a school district must contract. A competitive marketplace requires many providers. At this point, it remains unclear whether contracts will be signed with one, a few, or many. In many districts, contracts are currently being signed with only one or a few providers.

Contract negotiations

Federal regulations provide local districts with a great deal of latitude when negotiating contracts with providers, giving rise to conflicts between districts and providers. School districts must tell parents about free tutoring, contract with providers, and evaluate the program. But as Casserly tells us, the devil is in the details:

> School districts and potential providers have found themselves tussling over the length of the contracts, per pupil fees, billing and payment procedures, staff qualifications, union rules, and the like. . . .
>
> Many providers would like to receive a portion of their fees before work begins, but the districts often prefer to pay as the work proceeds. The providers would like to charge the districts a flat fee for the number of students enrolled in the tutorial sessions. The districts think they should be charged only for the number of students who actually attend the instructional sessions. The providers would like to build transportation fees into their overhead charges, but the districts generally disallow these expenses because the law does not authorize them. Some providers would like to provide their services on school grounds, while the districts want the option to charge for use of the facilities.[73]

Thus districts have incentives to write contracts that impose challenges for providers. As an administrator in Worcester explained, "We're not required to provide transportation. And, to be honest, to send money out of the district, I'm not sure that we would even offer to do that."[74]

Summary and Recommendations

It is too early to tell whether the free tutoring provision of NCLB will become a dynamic part of school reform or whether it will be absorbed into the existing institutional structure. On the one hand, participation in the free tutoring program is growing more rapidly than is the school-choice program. On the other hand, districts have incentives to limit participation or to simply offer the services themselves, especially if no accountability provisions are put into place. To ensure greater program effectiveness, I recommend that the law be strengthened in the following ways:

1. The certification of providers should be administered by a state agency other than the state department of education. And the local school district should not be the primary contractor for tutoring or other supplemental services.
2. To avoid conflicts of interest, a new agency should certify and sign contracts with providers, who would then have the authority to offer services to all eligible students within the state. This agency should then make available to providers the names and contact information of all eligible students and their families. Providers should be given the opportunity to contact these families directly. The agency should have the responsibility for evaluating services provided.
3. The new agency should employ parent advocates that will help them identify and assess appropriate providers of supplemental services.
4. Funds available for free tutoring and other supplemental services, if unused, should return to the federal Treasury, not to school districts, so that incentives for nonparticipation are removed.
5. If school districts continue to have the authority to contract out for tutoring services, regulations should ensure that a level playing field is established. Further, contracts should be signed with multiple providers, so that parents have a choice among services. No provider should be refused on either the grounds that they are faith-based or that they are a for-profit firm.
6. Tutoring providers should be held accountable for student performance. That they are not is an anomaly in a law designed to achieve greater accountability. Scores on state accountability exams of students who are tutored should be examined to see whether these students are making gains.

Notes

1. Matt Chingos and Mark Linnen provided research assistance for this chapter.
2. James Peyser and Robert Costrell, "Exploring the Costs of Accountability," *Education Next* 4, no. 3 (summer 2004): 23–31.
3. Andrew Rudalevig, "No Child Left Behind: Forging a Congressional Compromise," in *No Child Left Behind? The Politics and Practice of Accountability,* eds. Paul E. Peterson and Martin West (Washington, D.C.: Brookings Institution, 2003): 23–54.
4. Ronald Brownstein, "Implementing No Child Left Behind," in *The Future of School Choice,* ed. Paul E. Peterson (Stanford, Calif.: Hoover Institution Press, 2003): 216.
5. Jen Sansbury, "Obstacles Hold Kids in Bad Schools," *Atlanta Journal Constitution,* September 15, 2002; Mary MacDonald, "School Transfer Rush Is On," *Atlanta Journal Constitution,* August 2, 2002.
6. Tricia Bishop, "Few Use School Transfer Option," *Baltimore Sun,* October 24, 2003.
7. William Howell, "One Child at a Time," *Education Next* 4, no. 3 (summer 2004): 26–31.
8. Bishop, "Few Use School Transfer Option"; Linda Perlstein, "Child's Fate, Between the Lines," *Washington Post,* June 23, 2003; Curtis Lawrence and Chreyl L. Reed, "Few Kids Eligible, Fewer Join in School Transfer Program," *Chicago Sun-Times,* September 26, 2003.
9. Michael Casserly, "No Child Left Behind: A Status Report on Choice and Supplemental Services in America's Great City Schools," paper presented at Conference on Public School Choice and Supplemental Service Provisions of No Child Left Behind, American Enterprise Institute–Thomas B. Fordham Institute (Washington, D.C., January 2004).
10. Sherry Parmet, "Tickets to Better School Unclaimed," *San Diego Union-Tribune,* April 11, 2004, B-1: Center on Education Policy, *From the Capital to the Classroom: Year 2 of the No Child Left Behind Act* (Washington, D. C.: Center on Education Policy, 2004): 89.
11. Center on Education Policy, *From the Capitol to the Classroom,* 89.
12. Parmet, "Tickets to Better School Unclaimed," B-1.
13. Tricia Bishop, "Transfer Option Perplexes Schools," *Baltimore Sun,* May 23, 2004.
14. Jen Sansbury, "DeKalb Student Transfers Increase Nearly Sevenfold," *Atlanta Journal-Constitution,* October 9, 2003, 8JA.

15. Jennifer Smith Richards, "Columbus Schools: Transfer Requests Jump Dramatically," *Columbus Dispatch*, May 7, 2004, 1A.

16. Rosalind Rossi, "Early Results on 'No Child': Progress," *Chicago Sun-Times*, April 25, 2004, 10.

17. Elissa Gootman, "New York Will Eliminate Free Pass Out of Failing Schools," *New York Times*, July 17, 2004, A11.

18. Richards, "Columbus Schools," 1A.

19. Center on Education Policy, *From the Capitol to the Classroom*, 90, Table 3-B.

20. Rossi, "Early Results on 'No Child,'" 10.

21. Casserly, "No Child Left Behind."

22. Richards, "Columbus Schools," 1A.

23. Terry M. Moe, *Schools, Vouchers, and the American Public* (Washington, D.C.: Brookings Institution, 2001).

24. William Howell, "Parents, Choice and NCLB's Future," paper presented at Conference on Public School Choice and Supplemental Service Provisions of No Child Left Behind, American Enterprise Institute–Thomas B. Fordham Institute (Washington, D. C., January 2004).

25. Howell, "Parents, Choice."

26. Howell, "Parents, Choice": Peter Simon, "Parents Unaware of Right to Leave Deficient Schools," *Buffalo News*, February 5, 2003; Brighter Choice Public School Choice Project, "Press Release: Survey of Buffalo Parents" (Albany, New York), January 22, 2003.

27. Howell, "Parents, Choice."

28. William Howell and Paul E. Peterson, with Patrick Wolf and David Campbell, *The Education Gap: Vouchers and Urban Schools* (Washington, D.C.: Brookings Institution, 2002).

29. Gootman, "New York Will Eliminate Free Pass," A11.

30. NCLB provisions sometimes come into conflict with court-ordered or state desegregation policies. In Virginia, schools in Richmond and Walton counties say they must adhere to court orders to desegregate, precluding them from approving transfer requests (Sansbury, "Obstacles Hold Kids in Bad Schools"). Similarly in Worcester, Massachusetts, school officials invoked state laws requiring racial de-isolation of students as a reason for refusing transfers (Howell, "One Child").

31. Casserly, "No Child Left Behind."

32. Julian R. Betts and Anne Danenberg, "Too Many Cooks Spoil the Broth? The Implementation of No Child Left Behind in San Diego," paper presented at Conference on Public School Choice and Supplemental Service Provisions of No Child Left Behind, American Enterprise Institute–Thomas B. Fordham Institute (Washington, D. C., January 2004): 19.

33. Ibid., 29.

34. Center on Education Policy, *From the Capitol to the Classroom*, 83.

35. Howell, "Parents, Choice."

36. Betts and Danenberg, "Too Many Cooks Spoil the Broth?" 34.

37. Ibid.

38. Casserly, "No Child Left Behind."

39. Howell, "One Child at a Time," 13.

40. Ibid., 10–11.

41. Ibid.

42. Sansbury, "Obstacles Hold Kids in Bad Schools."

43. Howard Week, "Columbia Rules Limit Fee Phase-in," *Baltimore Sun*, August 24, 2003.

44. Center on Education Policy, *From the Capitol to the Classroom*, 94.

45. U. S. Department of Education, "Key Policy Letters Signed by the Education Secretary or Deputy Secretary," June 14, 2002, at http:www.ed.gov./policy/elsec/guid/secletter/020614.html.

46. Betts and Danenberg, "Too Many Cooks Spoil the Broth?" 33.

47. Elissa Gootman, "New York City's Schools Fear a Wave of Transfers," *New York Times*, September 30, 2003.

48. Rossi, "Early Results on 'No Child,'" 8.

49. Gootman, "New York Will Eliminate Free Pass," A11.

50. Caroline M. Hoxby, "What Has Changed and What Has Not," in *Our Schools and Our Future: Are We Still at Risk?* ed. Paul E. Peterson (Stanford, Calif.: Hoover Institution Press, 2003): 73–110.

51. Siobhan Gorman, "The Invisible Hand of No Child Left Behind," paper presented at Conference on Public School Choice and Supplemental Service Provisions of No Child Left Behind, American Enterprise Institute–Thomas B. Fordham Institute (Washington, D.C., January 2004), p. 9. Also see Siobhan Gorman, "Selling Supplemental Services," *Education Next* 4, no. 4 (Fall 2004): 30–36.

52. Gorman, "Invisible Hand."

53. Casserly, "No Child Left Behind."

54. Tanya Sierra, "Few Taking Free Tutorings," *Press Enterprise* (Riverside, Calif.), May 17, 2004, A1.

55. Lisa Connors, "A Harder Look at After-School Help," *Christian Science Monitor*, January 27, 2004.

56. Deirdre Fernandes, "Tutors Are Ready—and Waiting," *Virginian-Pilot* (Norfolk, Virginia), February 21, 2004, B1.

57. Sarah Carr, "Results Mixed for City Tutoring Venture," *Milwaukee Journal Sentinel*, May 10, 2004, 1B.

58. Center on Education Policy, *From the Capitol to the Classroom*, 107.

59. Gorman, "Invisible Hand."

60. Fernandes, "Tutors Are Ready," B1.

61. Center on Education Policy, *From the Capitol to the Classroom*, 110. The frank statement was probably due to the anonymity given the spokesperson by the researchers.

62. Rick Karlin, "Bold Step in Learning in a City Living Room," *Times Union* (Albany, New York), April 28, 2004, A1.

63. Sierra, "Few Taking Free Tutoring," A1.

64. Ibid.

65. Gorman, "Invisible Hand."

66. Howell, "One Child at a Time," 19.

67. Center on Education Policy, *From the Capitol to the Classroom*, 110.

68. Casserly, "No Child Left Behind."

69. Betts and Danenberg, "Too Many Cooks Spoil the Broth?" 22.

70. Carr, "Results Mixed for City Tutoring Venture," 1B.

71. Gorman, "Invisible Hand."

72. Ibid.

73. Casserly, "No Child Left Behind."

74. Howell, "One Child at a Time," 19.

8

A Highly Qualified Teacher in Every Classroom

Terry M. Moe

The No Child Left Behind (NCLB) Act is best known as a landmark effort by the federal government to hold the public schools accountable for their performance through rigorous standards and tests. But it does much more than that. In a move just as unprecedented as its new accountability system, NCLB requires that all academic courses in every public school be taught by "highly qualified" teachers—and it specifies what "highly qualified" means. For the first time in American history, the federal government is telling the states who can teach in the public schools.

In a culture that prizes local democracy, such a move raises all kinds of issues. But judged purely by its goal of improving student achievement, NCLB would appear to be on solid ground in pushing for higher quality teachers. A good deal of research now shows that, among all the factors that policymakers can arguably hope to influence, teacher quality is probably the single most important determinant of how much students learn.[1] This being so, a successful effort to raise teacher quality could have big payoffs in raising the academic achievement of the nation's children. And more than that, were such a reform to bring high quality teachers to the most disadvantaged districts, as NCLB fully intends, it could help narrow the achievement gaps that have long plagued American education.

Good ideas don't automatically translate into good policy, however, and the question remains whether the requirements written into NCLB will actually work on the ground. Will the states respond by putting teachers into the classroom who are truly well qualified? And will disadvantaged districts come to have teachers who are just as qualified as those in districts that are well off? The answers can't be known with any certainty at this point, but there are good reasons for believing that the act— if unmodified—will promote only modest improvements in these respects and fall short of its goals.

In this chapter I explain why this is so and discuss some of the problems involved in NCLB's attempt to mandate better teachers. I go on to suggest some midcourse corrections that, if adopted, may allow the act to achieve its goals more effectively.

The Mandate

NCLB requires that all teachers of core academic subjects be highly qualified by the 2005–2006 school year, and that in programs receiving Title I money (targeted at disadvantaged children) all newly hired teachers of core academic subjects be highly qualified by 2002–2003.[2] Teachers are regarded as highly qualified when they

- have a bachelor's degree from a four-year institution
- have full state certification
- demonstrate competence in the subject matter that they teach.

The requirement of subject-matter competence is the great innovation of this mandate. The states already require certification and bachelor's degrees, but they often do not require demonstrations of substantive competence; when they do, as I discuss later, the demonstrations don't amount to much.[3] NCLB is an explicit attempt to get the states to do a better job of assuring that teachers know what they are teaching. Toward this end, it sets out new rules specifying how teacher competence must be demonstrated:

- New elementary school teachers must demonstrate competence by taking rigorous tests in math, reading, writing, and other components of the elementary curriculum.
- New middle school and high school teachers must demonstrate competence by passing rigorous exams in the subjects they teach, by having undergraduate or graduate degrees in those fields, by earning course credits equivalent to a college major, or by getting an advanced certificate or credential.
- Veteran teachers can demonstrate competence in the same ways that new teachers do. Or they can do it by meeting a "high, objective, uniform state standard of evaluation" (HOUSSE), which the states devise on their own. Whatever specific methods and criteria the states decide to use, their new HOUSSE systems must: be grade-appropriate, be aligned with state academic standards, be developed in consultation with educators, provide objective and coherent information about teacher competence, and be applied uniformly to all teachers in the same subjects and grade levels. HOUSSE systems may also take into consideration (but not be primarily based on) the number of years the teacher has been teaching.[4]

Problems of Top-Down Control

This might seem to be a simple mandate that is well suited to effective implementation by the states. But it actually isn't. Fundamental problems get in the way—problems that could have been anticipated before the legislation was even written.

Measurability

Teacher quality is difficult to measure. What the architects of NCLB want the states to do, of course, is to fill their classrooms with good teachers who can succeed at getting students to learn. But there is no objective method for identifying which people are good teachers and which are not.

One possibility, at least in principle, is that teacher quality be evaluated by reference to student test scores. But achievement tests can measure only part of what students are expected to know; they measure it with error; and their outcomes are influenced by all sorts of other factors—especially the social backgrounds of the kids—that make it difficult to partial out how much learning can be attributed to a given teacher.[5] This approach is also anathema to teachers and their unions, who oppose using test scores to evaluate teacher quality.[6]

A much easier alternative, both practically and politically, is to focus on characteristics of the teachers themselves: whether they are certified, how long they have been teaching, their college majors and degrees, their ability to pass tests of competence, their SAT scores, and the like. These proxies for teacher quality are even more removed from the learning outcomes that good teaching is supposed to produce, and they do an imperfect job of measuring true quality. But they are readily observed, they provide an objective basis for making judgments about quality— and the authors of NCLB really didn't have much choice but to go this route, assuming they wanted to be in the business of telling the states which teachers are good enough to hire. They are in good company, at any rate, because virtually all policymakers, researchers, and educators use these proxies as well.

Some proxies are better than others, though. The standard measure of teacher quality employed by the states is certification, and the fact that almost all teachers are certified is supposed to give Americans confidence that teachers are of high quality. Another standard measure is the advanced college degree: 52 percent of teachers now have at least a master's degree, and these teachers are paid more than those with bachelor's degrees because they are alleged to be of higher quality.[7] Academic research has never shown, however, that these teacher characteristics have an appreciable affect on how much students learn.[8] Research does show, on the other hand, that the cognitive abilities (as measured by objective tests) and substantive knowledge of teachers (as measured by either college majors or by tests) are determinants of student achievement.[9]

Judging by these research-supported proxies, there is reason to worry about the current level of teacher quality in this nation. It is clear, for example, that the people who go into public school teaching are themselves not among the best students, at least on average, and that their cognitive abilities are not what a quality school system requires. On the SAT and ACT tests, the nation's most widely used measures of cognitive ability at the college level, most students who plan to go into teaching are drawn from the lower end of the distribution.[10] By contrast, private school teachers—who typically don't have to be certified at all—are considerably higher in average cognitive ability. Thirty-three percent of them score in the top quartile on these tests, compared to just 14 percent of those certified to teach in the public schools.[11]

The evidence also suggests that, all too often, public school teachers are not sufficiently competent in the subjects they teach. A reasonable proxy for substantive knowledge is whether teachers have academic majors in the fields they teach, and by this measure there is clearly a problem. Some 78 percent of elementary school teachers do not have an academic major, with most simply majoring in education, where programs typically emphasize pedagogy and other topics that have no demonstrated impact on student performance. Even in secondary schools, the percentage of teachers who don't have majors in the fields they teach is quite high: approximately 50 percent of teachers in English, 53 percent in math, 45 percent in science, and 45 percent in social studies.[12]

Of course, some of these teachers without majors may well be competent. Indeed, at the time NCLB was passed, thirty-two states required a test of substantive competence as one of the requirements for certification, and a fair portion of the teachers without majors in their subjects have presumably passed such tests and thereby "demonstrated" competence.[13] But the problem is that these tests, much like the general certification tests that teachers typically take—and that 93 percent currently pass—are often pitched at a very low academic level and are not rigorous enough to measure true competence. To make matters worse, the passing bar may be set so low that even a poor score on an easy test is sufficient, ensuring that many people who are quite mediocre can make it through and gain certification to teach those subjects, especially after taking the tests multiple times.[14] When the tests are rigorous and the passing bars set at a reasonable level, some teachers do miserably. In Philadelphia, for instance, where veteran middle school teachers were recently required to take tests of substantive competence, almost two-thirds of the math teachers failed the math test and 53 percent of the science teachers failed the science test.[15]

A good case can be made, then, that America's teachers are not of sufficiently high quality on average and that NCLB is attacking a problem that is both real and important. We have to recognize, however, that the true quality of the nation's teachers has not been measured with great accuracy and that the depth and breadth of the problem are not well understood. We are judging on the basis of proxies, and the proxies are quite imperfect. Clearly, many teachers without a college major in math can do an excellent job of teaching algebra or geometry. And many who can pass an exam in English or history may be incapable of communicating the material to students or inspiring them to learn. Proxies for good teaching are *not the same* as good teaching. They can give only an approximation—a measure with error—of any given teacher's true quality. And they can give only an approximation of the overall quality of the teaching pool.

NCLB inherits these same problems. Its mandate is an attempt to require high-quality teachers in every classroom. But because it can't require this in concrete terms, it requires it in terms of proxies: teachers must have college majors or be able to pass certain exams. Even if the act is carried out faithfully and effectively by the states, therefore, they won't necessarily be putting good teachers into classrooms. They will be relying on teachers who have college majors or can pass exams, and these people may or may not be good teachers. Presumably, given the research literature, the quality of the entire pool of teachers would increase were these proxies seriously adhered to, and student achievement would improve as well. But there will still be many other, unaccounted-for factors that influence whether teachers are really doing a good job, and there will still be plenty of people who meet the formal criteria but are lousy teachers—which can only limit the achievement gains. And this, sad to say, is pretty much the best-case scenario, for it assumes that the act is faithfully and effectively executed.

Politics

State policymakers could have designed rigorous tests of teacher competence if they had wanted to years ago, but most states simply didn't do it. They purposely designed tests that were too easy, knowing full well what they were doing. Similarly, they could have required that teachers have an academic major, but most states didn't do that either. Instead, they have largely relied on education schools to determine what teachers ought to know in preparation for jobs in the classroom; and the ed schools, which are firmly in the grip of "progressive" pedagogical ideas (in which learning is child-centered and teachers are "facilitators"), have never regarded the subject matter knowledge of teachers as a top priority.[16]

Why would state policymakers go this route? Why wouldn't they do whatever it took, on their own, to create systems that produce the highest quality teachers possible? The answers are fundamentally political, and they have a lot to tell us about what we can expect when the states are relied on to implement NCLB.

The states are not lackeys of the federal government, eager to follow its mandates. They are political systems in their own right, governed by elected public officials who are concerned about their own reelection and responsive to powerful groups in their constituencies. When it comes to education policy, the groups that often have the greatest clout with public officials are those with vested interests in public education—notably the teachers unions, but also the education schools and associations of administrators and school boards.

These are precisely the groups whose interests are most threatened by NCLB, including its provisions for highly qualified teachers. The teachers unions are in the business of protecting member jobs, and they would like to ensure that *all* of their members are deemed highly qualified—and remain employed. The education schools stay in business by certifying teachers, so they oppose policies by which teachers could become certified without graduating from an ed school, and they oppose rigorous tests that large numbers of their graduates might fail. Administrators and school board members are responsible for finding teachers to fill their classrooms, and they oppose new requirements that make it more difficult to do that, especially when many districts are already complaining of teacher shortages.[17]

There is also political pressure in support of NCLB, of course, often coming from business groups that favor accountability and want to see the act administered effectively. But these groups have a broad array of political concerns, and they are not nearly as focused on NCLB—or as willing to invest political resources doing battle over it—as the teachers unions and other vested interests are. So at the end of the day, state officials often have political incentives to depart from faithful execution of the mandate, and to resist making major (threatening) changes to established rules and institutions. Because implementation is costly, moreover, they may have financial reasons for holding back as well.

Reformers have two rays of hope, however. The first is that accountability is popular with the electorate at large, and politicians—even many Democrats allied with the education establishment—have incentives to show that they support it. This goes a long way toward explaining why NCLB was adopted in the first place, despite the opposition of powerful education groups, and why so many states have been able to adopt their own accountability systems.[18] The second ray of hope arises from the first. Now that NCLB and many state accountability systems have actually been adopted, the public spotlight on school performance—and thus test scores—may give public officials stronger electoral incentives to put teachers who are truly well qualified in every classroom.

It's all a matter of degree, of course, and the balance of pressures and incentives will vary from state to state. The bottom line, nonetheless, is that the federal government cannot count on having NCLB implemented faithfully and aggressively by state-level agents who are fully on board. State officials are products of their own political systems, responsive to political pressures, and to some extent—perhaps a very great extent—likely to resist the kinds of changes NCLB calls for.

Finally, it is important to add that the federal government cannot even count on *itself* to push for effective implementation of the law, because its own motivations are sensitive to politics too. The Department of Education, which is in charge of administering NCLB, is the target of heavy political pressures from congressional critics, education groups, and state and local officials to go easy on the states, to grant them flexibility, to put up with delays, and not to apply sanctions (like withholding money) when the states fail to act. These pressures have only intensified since the act's adoption, as important Democrats—many of whom voted for NCLB—have swung back into line with their longtime establishment allies and are now portraying the act as overly burdensome and intrusive.[19] For the department to act aggressively under these circumstances is to invite a firestorm, so there is good political reason for them to hold back and be nice.

Information

If NCLB is to be well implemented, good information is essential. State officials must have sufficient information to do their jobs effectively, assuming this is what they want to do. And because they may *not* want to do it, good information about what state officials are actually doing must be available to the federal government, so that compliance can be monitored and capabilities assessed. Poor information on either count can seriously undermine the prospects for effective implementation. And we have every reason to expect problems on both.[20]

With so much of public education concentrated at the local level, most information is local. State governments require reports from their school districts, especially on how money gets spent and how categorical programs are operated. But this is only a partial remedy, and most information about schools, students, and teachers remains highly decentralized and unavailable to state officials. It is not even clear, moreover, that the districts are in any position to provide it. Historically, they have been organized to manage schools and educate kids, not to create vast data banks on every aspect of their operations. So even if they wanted to help out, most districts would have limited information to pass on, and different districts would have different types and amounts. There is no comprehensive information system that state officials can tie into, and certainly not one that is uniform across the states.[21]

The lack of information clearly hinders their capacity for effective action. How are the states supposed to put a highly qualified teacher in every classroom if they don't even know how many of their current teachers are highly qualified, or which ones? Lacking this kind of basic information, they can't know what kinds of problems they face or what kinds of resources or strategies are most appropriate for solving them. Even if politics were not an issue, therefore, and state officials were purely dedicated to the implementation of NCLB, they would hardly be in a position to do it well.

A second information problem arises because much of what the states actually do in implementing the act—or not—may be difficult or impossible for the Department of Education to observe. It can try to remedy this by requiring detailed reports. But reports are filled with information that the states themselves provide. And not only is the states' information likely to be spotty and unreliable, but they also have incentives to manipulate the information they provide in ways that promote their own self-interest—by giving the impression, for example, that they are trying hard to comply when they are really not. The numbers in a report may have the look of hard, objective data. But they can be also meaningless or misleading. Even if they aren't, the information in reports is just the tip of a very large iceberg and cannot tell the department everything it needs to know.

Because information is likely to be such a large problem for the department, states that want to resist NCLB's mandates needn't do anything so provocative as refusing to comply with the law. They can give the appearance of acting in good faith, and the department may have no good way of knowing what they are actually doing or how well they are doing it. Moreover, the fact that the states themselves are likely to have poor information means that they can claim that some of what NCLB requires simply isn't possible given current capabilities. In some cases, this may be legitimate. But because the department does not have full access to the states' own information, it can't know whether the states are truly incapable, or to what extent and in what areas, and so will have a hard time judging why the states are not doing an effective job.

As this discussion only begins to suggest, when the information problem is combined with the political problem, the implications for NCLB are troubling. The states have political incentives not to carry out the law faithfully and effectively; but they also have access to key information that the federal government does not have, and they can put this asymmetry to use in failing to carry out the law. Information is necessary if the states are to do a good job, but it is also a weapon they can employ to *avoid* doing a good job; and the federal government will have a difficult time doing anything about it—or even telling the difference between the two.

The Reality of Top-Down Control

NCLB went into effect in January 2002, and at this writing has been on the books for almost three years. During this time, all fifty states have been busy responding and reacting to the countless new requirements of the act, including the requirements for teacher quality, and the Department of Education has been busy monitoring them, collecting reports, issuing clarifying regulations, and giving advice. The sheer level of activity has been extraordinarily high. But what really seems to be going on? And how effectively are the teacher-quality provisions of the act being implemented?

This is what Senators Edward Kennedy and Jeff Bingaman were wondering when, in an early attempt to get feedback on implementation, they asked the General Accounting Office (GAO) to conduct a study on what the states were doing to put high quality teachers in the classroom. When the GAO reported back in July 2003, a year and a half after implementation had begun, its lead finding pointed to precisely the sort of information problem that an astute observer should have expected from the outset.

> We could not develop reliable data on the number of highly qualified teachers because states did not have the information needed to determine whether all teachers met the criteria. . . . Also, states did not have the information they needed to develop methods to evaluate subject area knowledge of their current teachers. . . . [Additionally] they did not have the data systems that could track teacher qualification by subject, which they needed to determine if a highly qualified teacher taught each core subject.[22]

In other words, the information problem was so severe that the states did not know enough to be able to carry out their jobs. And because the states lacked this information, the GAO itself did not have enough information to figure out what was going on, and how well the goals of the act were being realized. Everyone was basically in the dark.

A few months after the GAO report appeared, the states were faced with a deadline for filing reports with the Department of Education. In these reports, they were to provide data on the percentage of classrooms (statewide, as well as in low-performing districts) being taught by high-quality teachers. If the GAO is correct, states lack the information to provide accurate figures on these scores. Nonetheless, all but seven states submitted their reports as required. Here is an overview of the results:[23]

1. The figures that most states supplied were remarkably upbeat and positive. Thirty-one states claimed that more than 80 percent of their core classes were taught by highly qualified teachers, and twenty of these states put the figure at over 90 percent. For Wisconsin, it was 98.6 percent.

2. In thirty-one of forty-one states with data on low-performing districts, the percentage of classes taught by high-quality teachers in these districts was within just 5 percent of the statewide average. And in sixteen of these states, the percentage for low-performing districts was actually greater than or equal to the statewide average.
3. The numbers supplied by some states (a distinct minority) were starkly different on both these dimensions. Alaska, for instance, claimed that only 16 percent of its classrooms had high-quality teachers, Alabama put its figure at 35 percent, California at 48 percent. Similarly, some states claimed that their low-performing districts were well below the state average in having high-quality teachers in the classroom. Maryland reported that its low-performing districts were nearly 20 percent below the average, and California reported a 13 percent difference.

What are we to make of these figures? Are most states really so well stocked with highly qualified teachers that they come close to meeting the NCLB mandate out of the starting blocks? Is Alaska really so bad and Wisconsin so good when it comes to the quality of their teachers? Are teachers in California and Maryland really so inequitably distributed across districts by comparison to other states? And are we really prepared to believe that, in many states, low-performing districts have better teachers in the classroom than other districts do?

The Education Trust, a nonprofit organization dedicated to improving education for disadvantaged children, has been actively monitoring the implementation of NCLB, and it was quick to point out that these figures are not to be believed, and indeed that some have been manipulated to put states in a good light.

Some states appear to have taken the reporting provisions to heart. . . . But others took a different track. Some states simply didn't report any data, citing an inability to gather even this most basic information. And some states seem to have used their discretion in interpreting the law to cross the line that separates fact from fiction, to paint a rosy picture that is simply

186 / Terry M. Moe

at odds with reality. In this last group of states, the numbers reported on September 1 border on farce and veer into tragedy.[24]

The fact is, much of the information provided by state officials is meaningless and can't be taken at face value. In part, this is because the states suffer from major information problems. But even if they didn't, they would still be unable to provide meaningful responses. This is because large percentages of veteran teachers do not have majors in the fields they are teaching or have not passed an exam that NCLB would consider adequate, and they can only be categorized as highly qualified if they meet the HOUSSE standards that the states are supposed to devise for evaluating them.[25] But at the time of the reports, many states had not even formulated these standards, so they couldn't possibly have had any idea how many of their veterans might be qualified. And even in states that had formulated their HOUSSE standards, veteran teachers had yet to be evaluated, and there was no way of knowing how the evaluations would come out. So where did the figures in their reports come from? They were essentially discretionary numbers, and state officials made their own determinations—different in different states—about how to calculate them.

In most cases, given the rosy picture that predominates in these reports, the underlying presumption of state officials seems to have been that *all* veteran teachers are already highly qualified—based on their majors or on existing certification requirements—or that they will eventually be highly qualified, once the new rules and criteria are in place. In other words, there is no indication that state officials expect any veteran teachers to lose their jobs for reasons of competence. This is consistent, of course, with the political pressures they are under from the teachers unions and other education groups, which want to ensure that no one loses a job, that everyone is labeled highly qualified, and that life goes on with as few disruptions as possible.

Grandfathering in all veteran teachers would obviously violate the most fundamental intentions of NCLB. But the opportunities for such grandfathering are contained within NCLB itself, for its HOUSSE provisions create a loophole big enough to drive three million teachers through. NCLB gives the states a great deal of flexibility in designing their own standards for evaluating veteran teachers, and the states have strong political incentives to use this flexibility to create standards that all veterans can satisfy, even if some portion of them are not knowledgeable enough to be in the classroom.

Since the state reports were submitted, more states have firmed up their HOUSSE standards, and we now have a reasonable picture of what they are doing on this score. The picture isn't a pretty one. As *Education Week* noted, "States have fashioned wildly different ways of judging whether teachers already in the classroom meet the federal standard,"[26] so what highly qualified means in one state may have nothing to do with what it means in another state. What most of them have in common, however, is that they put the emphasis on criteria that do *not* demonstrate substantive competence, but guarantee that veteran teachers will be labeled highly qualified. Depending on the state, teachers can meet the new standards through some combination of teacher experience, classroom evaluations, portfolios, professional development, college coursework, and the states' existing credentialing criteria. Consider the following examples:[27]

- In Arkansas, teachers with five years' experience automatically satisfy the standard.
- In California, Florida, Washington, and West Virginia, teachers are classified as highly qualified if they receive satisfactory evaluations of their classroom performance based on observations by supervisors (or submit acceptable portfolios)—the usual way teachers are evaluated anyway. The criteria for these evaluations include the usual laundry list—communication skills, class climate, and the like—and do not put a premium on substantive knowledge.
- In New Hampshire, teachers can meet the standard if they engage in a "self-assessment" with a competent "partner" and put together evidence (via portfolios and the like) showing their supervisors that they have the necessary substantive knowledge.

- In Ohio and Massachusetts, teachers can become highly qualified by racking up enough hours in professional development activities.
- In Indiana, Montana, Nebraska, South Dakota, and Wisconsin, the existing systems for licensing teachers in the relevant subjects are taken as the HOUSSE standards, which means that all teachers with the appropriate licenses are automatically highly qualified.
- In Alabama, California, New York, Ohio, and a number of other states, HOUSSE standards are met through a system that allocates points for various criteria, such as classroom performance, experience, portfolios, and the like. In most cases, experience counts heavily. In almost all cases, any teacher can easily accumulate the required number of points. New York, for example, requires 100 points to meet the standard, but it awards 30 points just for a bachelor's degree with a general education component, up to 50 points for experience (10 points a year), and points for professional development and related activities.

As these examples suggest, the problem is pervasive and not confined to a few wayward states. The National Council on Teacher Quality, a reform group that seeks to promote better teaching, carried out an in-depth study of the HOUSSE standards of twenty randomly selected states and gave each state a grade based upon how well their standards met even the most basic NCLB criteria—for example, that the standards provide rigorous, objective evidence of teacher knowledge and help identify teachers who are not competent. Only Illinois received an A. The vast majority of states received a C, D, or F, yielding an average grade of D+ across all twenty states. The situation the report describes is a sorry one indeed.

> States getting low marks appear unwilling to address a problem that plagues the nation as a whole and seem to believe that "business as usual" is an appropriate response. States have also proved wildly inventive at coming up with an array of activities that are supposed indicators of teaching subject matter

knowledge, but which can at best be said to bear only slight relation to such knowledge.[28]

The HOUSSE provisions are perhaps the most critical component of NCLB's implementation because they determine whether the three million teachers who currently occupy the nation's public school classrooms will be held to a high standard of substantive knowledge. With the states using the HOUSSE provisions as a loophole to safeguard jobs, however, even the most incompetent teachers will remain in the system for years to come, many of them for decades, and NCLB's goal of upgrading the teaching force will be seriously compromised. For the foreseeable future, the act cannot succeed if the states insist on a charade in which every veteran teacher is highly qualified.

In the longer term, though, there are grounds for hope in the requirements NCLB sets out for *new* teachers. People who want to enter the teaching force must have college majors in the subjects they teach or be able to pass rigorous tests that demonstrate their substantive knowledge. For now these requirements are not as critical as the HOUSSE requirements because they apply to a much smaller number of people. But over time these (formerly) new teachers will constitute an increasing proportion of the teaching pool, and eventually they will make up all of it. So if the NCLB standards for new recruits are truly rigorous and effectively imposed—and if we are willing to wait long enough—the average quality of U.S. teachers could well be raised in significant fashion, as the act intends.

But are the standards for new teachers being designed and implemented in ways that would generate a future surge in quality? There is a good deal of confusion about what the states are doing on this score. The Education Commission of the States, which keeps a running tally of state activities related to NCLB, says that forty-three states have authorized tests for new elementary teachers, that four appear to be in the process of doing so, and that four are not. On the surface, these numbers seem promising—although there is no justification, after two years, for not getting 100 percent compliance. Yet the numbers on what the states are doing with regard to subject matter tests, which are especially relevant for middle and high school teachers, are not even promising on the surface: only eleven have authorized such tests, thirty-eight appear to be in the process of doing so, and two aren't.[29]

What do these numbers really mean? In the first place, they don't mean that the states actually have real tests in place and are using them—only that they have authorized such tests. The numbers also don't indicate whether the states are developing new tests specifically for NCLB or just using tests that they have used in the past; indeed, as I pointed out in the HOUSSE analysis above, a number of states are just using their preexisting tests. More important, though, the numbers say nothing about the *content* of the tests or the level of performance required to get a passing score—and thus say nothing about whether the tests are well suited for ensuring that prospective teachers actually know their subject matter. There is good reason, given the states' past experiences with the design and adoption of tests, to worry that these new tests and passing bars will *not* in fact be rigorous and that they will fall short of NCLB's goals. There are political pressures from the education community to make these tests easy to pass, and there is no reason to think that state officials are suddenly going to require rigorous tests that large numbers of prospective teachers fail.

There are clearly some serious problems, then, with the way the act is being implemented by the states. It is the Department of Education's job to deal with these problems and to see that NCLB is implemented as effectively as possible. This is a difficult challenge, and many of the difficulties—which are due to the design of the act and to the vicissitudes of top-down control—have been thrust on the department from without and are obviously not its fault. Even so, the department has fallen short in certain respects.[30]

First, it has been slow in issuing clarifying regulations and other sorts of guidance. This is important, because NCLB is not sufficiently detailed for the states to know exactly what is expected of them. The states were already supposed to have put a highly qualified teacher in every Title 1 classroom by the fall of 2002—and the department didn't even issue its "final" clarifying regulations until November 2002, after the deadline had come and gone.[31]

Second, the department has not been proactive enough in dealing with data problems. It was obvious from the outset that the states didn't have the data systems to be able to file meaningful reports on their percentages of highly qualified teachers—and it certainly became apparent once the process was underway. Why allow them to file figures that are totally meaningless? At the very least, states could have been provided with clear guidelines as to how highly qualified teachers were to be identified and counted, and all states could have filed figures that had the same meaning. The fact that HOUSSE standards were not in place, and that veteran teachers could not be fully evaluated, should have been dealt with openly and clearly, so that all states could follow the same game plan in making their counts. As the Education Trust put it:[32]

> The federal government has a critical responsibility to serve as more than just a conduit for state-reported data of dubious value. It needs to provide clear guidance on what is required. It also needs to insist that the data meet basic standards of validity and reliability, and show a good-faith compliance with the letter and clear intent of the law. If states are unwilling to comply, the Department must take action. So far, the Department has simply refused to do so.

Third, the department has allowed states to eviscerate NCLB's requirements for highly qualified teachers by letting them adopt HOUSSE standards that make a mockery of the act's intentions and are even in clear violation of the wording of the law. The law requires that the HOUSSE standards be objective; but as we have seen, in many states they are not—they are based on subjective assessments of classroom performance, for example, or portfolios. The law says that the purpose of HOUSSE standards is to demonstrate subject matter competence, yet in most states a teacher can satisfy the adopted standards without demonstrating competence at all. And the law clearly does not want HOUSSE standards to put heavy emphasis on mere experience in the classroom, but in many states experience counts very heavily indeed, often 50 percent and sometimes more. The department could have stepped in, told states clearly and forcefully that such approaches were unacceptable, and *required* HOUSSE standards that really do demonstrate substantive competence. But instead it allowed the states to go their own ways.

Fourth, the department has done much the same when it comes to testing new teachers. There is no indication thus far that the department is in the business of evaluating state tests to determine if they are sufficiently rigorous or their passing bars sufficiently high. At this point, the mere fact that states *have* tests of substantive competence (or even just authorized them), and that teachers are required to take them, appears to be taken as prima facie evidence that they are on their way toward meeting the provisions of the act.

No one outside the department can know for sure why it has been so tolerant of state departures from the act's intent. But one factor is surely that the department, like the states, is subject to political pressure and sensitive to political hostility and criticism—and thus has good reason to resist imposing requirements on states that they don't want to meet. This doesn't explain why the department was slow in providing guidance or why it wasn't more proactive in regard to the collection and presentation of data. These may have been administrative failures that can be corrected. But the political incentives, and the deference to the states that goes along with them, are more serious. Politics is here to stay, and it seems to be preventing the department from taking the kind of leadership role that is necessary if the act is to be implemented effectively.

Recommendations

In two annual reports on what it calls the "highly qualified teachers challenge," the department outlines its own ideas on where reforms under NCLB ought to be headed. These ideas are genuinely impressive. The department is deeply critical of how the states have traditionally certified, tested, and prepared their teachers; it recognizes that the states are under political pressure from established education groups to keep doing things as they always have; and it does not expect reform to come easily. It also has a vision, a "new model" of how certification, testing, and teacher preparation might be reconstituted. And it has a plan for how to get there.[33]

The new model would allow teachers to get certified without graduating from an education school, thus breaking the ed school monopoly. Teachers could get certified by having the relevant college majors or passing challenging tests with sufficiently high scores. The states might have additional requirements, such as streamlined training programs or on-the-job mentoring, but the bureaucratic hurdles would be kept to a minimum. The idea is to maintain high standards but to radically reduce the current barriers to entry that now discourage many talented people from getting into the field.

The department's plan for getting states to move toward the new model turns on the not-coincidental fact that NCLB and its surrounding regulations *do not say* what the requirements for full certification are. The idea is that the states will find it difficult, given the size and quality of the current pool of candidates, to fulfill the NCLB mandate of a highly qualified teacher in every classroom—and will thus have incentives to take new approaches to certification that solve the problem. The states will have incentives, in other words, to *use* the flexibility built into the law to circumvent the education schools, to reduce bureaucratic hurdles, and to embrace something akin to the new model. As the department puts it:

> States have flexibility, then, to use this opportunity to think anew about their certification systems, and to consider major revisions to existing systems. If states want to, they can dramatically streamline their processes and create alternative routes to full state certification that target talented people who would be turned off by traditional preparation and certification programs. In other words, NCLB gives the green light to states that want to lower barriers to the teaching profession.[34]

The model the department is proposing here has also been proposed by others—notably Hess,[35] who has developed the ideas in some detail—and it does indeed represent a major improvement over the model that now prevails in the states. But the department is probably wrong in thinking that the states will use their flexibility to move toward the new model on their own. The existing model is not well entrenched by accident. It is protected by powerful interests, and state officials have strong political reasons for *not* using the flexibility built into NCLB to pursue serious reform. Moreover, the department has so far taken an indulgent approach toward the states in its enforcement of the act, and as a result the states are not going to find it difficult to put a teacher who is nominally qualified in every classroom. Almost any teacher who is alive and kicking will meet the standards.

What can be done, then, to get the states to fill their classrooms with teachers who really are highly qualified—and more generally, to get states to adopt reforms that conform in broad outline to the new model? If we assume, in all practicality, that the basic top-down framework of NCLB is going to be kept, the issue is one of how it can be modified so that the underlying intentions of the act can be realized more effectively. Here are some modifications that seem reasonable, given the goals of the act and the problems that need to be addressed.

1. Teachers should only be regarded as highly qualified if they have a bachelor's degree and meet one of the following criteria: they have a college major in their teaching field, they can pass rigorous tests of substantive competence in that field, or their ability to raise student performance on high-stakes tests can be demonstrated in the classroom through a statistically sound, value-added methodology.

2. The HOUSSE provisions of the current act should be dropped. If veteran teachers are unable to meet the above standards, no other "qualifications"—such as classroom experience, satisfactory course evaluations, professional development—should be allowed to serve as substitutes.

These teachers should simply not be allowed to teach the corresponding subjects—or to teach at all, as the case may be.

3. Any teacher who is highly qualified by the above standards should automatically be granted certification. This means, among other things, that graduation from an education school should not be necessary for certification.

4. Tests of substantive competence must be truly rigorous and demanding, examine the proper content, and set the passing bar at a level that represents mastery of the material. To ensure as much, there should be an external assessment of all state tests. The department, for example, might set up an independent body of experts (from universities, say) who are equipped to do the job. Or the states could use tests developed by certain private organizations, such as the American Board for Certification of Teacher Excellence, that in the department's view have met these high standards.

5. Funding, expertise, and guidance should be provided to the states in an aggressive effort to help them develop the kinds of data systems required to implement the act effectively. To some extent, these systems need to be uniform from state to state, so that all are collecting, using, and reporting the same information.

Again, these proposals assume that the top-down approach of NCLB is to be retained, and that the challenge is to modify its rules so that the federal government's goal of high-quality teaching—and establishing the new model—can be more effectively pursued. This is not to say, however, that the top-down approach itself is the best way to go in the grander scheme of things. After all, no central authority in the Silicon Valley dictates to technology firms exactly how they ought to be organized or whom they ought to be hiring, yet they manage—on their own—to be extraordinarily successful and productive, often by following very different organizational paths. The explanation for their success is that they operate in a highly competitive environment, which gives the leaders of each firm strong incentives to hire the very best employees, to weed out employees who don't perform, and in general to organize as efficiently as possible. Indeed, if any central authority tried to force them into a single organizational mold, they would be far less productive.

The same sort of logic applies to the public schools. If they were highly competitive—due, let's say, to a major expansion of charter schools and vouchers—then their leaders would have strong incentives to hire competent teachers and organize efficiently on their own, and any top-down effort by the federal government to force them to hire and organize in particular ways would tend to undermine rather than enhance their performance. In the long run, then, the best prescription for getting high-quality teachers and high performing schools is not to figure out a better set of rules for controlling the schools from above, but rather to move toward a more competitive system that gets the incentives right and relies on lower-level officials to make their own decisions based on their own needs, judgments, and specific situations.

As Keynes so appropriately remarked, however, in the long run we are all dead. We live in the short run, and for the foreseeable future the school system is not going to be competitive and the incentives are not going to be right. This being so, the federal government cannot decentralize decisions to the state and local levels—by letting them make their own HOUSSE standards, for example—and assume that the desired, performance-enhancing decisions will be made. They won't. The poor performance of states and districts over the last few decades, and the political pressures that reinforce it, already demonstrate as much. Under these conditions, some measure of top-down control makes good sense—and a modification of NCLB, along the lines set out here, seems a reasonable way to move forward.

Notes

1. William Sanders and J. Rivers, *Research Project Report: Cumulative and Residual Effects of Teachers on Future Student Academic Achievement* (Knoxville: University of Tennessee, Value Added Research and As-

sessment Center, 1996). S. P. Wright, S. P. Horn, and William L. Sanders, "Teacher and Classroom Context Effects on Student Achievement: Implications for Teacher Evaluation," *Journal of Personnel Evaluation in Education* 11 (1997): 57–67. Steven Rivkin, Eric Hanushek, and J. Kain, "Teachers, Schools, and Academic Achievement," (Cambridge, Mass.: National Bureau of Economic Research, 1998), Working Paper No. 6691. Dan D. Goldhaber, Dominic J. Brewer, and D. J. Anderson, "A Three Way Error Components Analysis of Educational Productivity," *Educational Economics* 7(3) (1999): 199–208.

2. Core academic subjects include English, reading or language arts, math, science, foreign language, civics and government, economics, arts, history, and geography. The act can be read in its entirety on the U.S. Department of Education's web site at www.ed.gov/policy/landing.jhtml?src=rt (accessed September 2004). For a nontechnical discussion of the act and its requirements for high-quality teachers, see Twanna LaTrice Hill, "No Child Left Behind Policy Brief: Teacher Quality," (Denver, Colo.: Education Commission of the States, 2002).

3. Ibid. See also U.S. Department of Education, "Meeting the Highly Qualified Teachers Challenge: The Secretary's Annual Report on Teacher Quality" (Washington, D.C., 2002).

4. The act also has provisions that, among other things, require "high quality professional development" and outline the conditions under which individuals who are not fully certified—but who are in the process of becoming certified and meeting the standards of substantive competence—can teach. I will not focus on these aspects of the act here.

5. Eric A. Hanushek and Margaret E. Raymond, "Lessons about the Design of State Accountability Systems," in *No Child Left Behind? The Politics and Practice of School Accountability*, eds. Paul E. Peterson and Martin R. West (Washington, D.C.: Brookings Institution, 2003).

6. "NEA 2001–2002 Resolutions," National Education Association (2002), at www.nea.org.

7. U.S. Department of Education 2002.

8. Dan D. Goldhaber and Dominic J. Brewer, "Does Teacher Certification Matter? High School Certification Status and Student Achievement," *Educational Evaluation and Policy Analysis* 22 (2000): 129–45. Kate Walsh, "Teacher Certification Reconsidered" (Baltimore, Md.: Abell Foundation, 2001).

9. Eric A. Hanushek, "Teacher Characteristics and Gains in Student Achievement: Estimation Using Micro Data," *American Economic Review* 61 (2) (1971): 280–88. Eric A. Hanuushek, "Throwing Money at Schools,"

Journal of Policy Analysis and Management 1 (1) (1981): 19–42. Ronald G. Ehrenberg and Dominic J. Brewer, "Did Teachers' Race and Verbal Ability Matter in the 1960s? *Coleman* Revisited" NBER Working Paper No. 4293 (1993). William J. Webster, "Selecting Effective Teachers," *Journal of Educational Research* 91 (4) (1988): 245–53. D. Monk, "Subject Area Preparation of Secondary Mathematics and Science Teachers and Student Achievement," *Economics of Education Review* 13 (1994): 125–45.

10. R. Henke, S. Gies, and J. Giambattista, "Out of the Lecture Hall and into the Classroom: 1992–93 College Graduates and Elementary/Secondary School Teaching" (Washington, D.C.: U.S. Department of Education, National Center for Education Statistics, 1996): 96-899. Dale Ballou, "Do Public Schools Hire the Best Applicants?" *Quarterly Journal of Economics* 111(1) (1996): 97–133.

11. U.S. Department of Education 2002.

12. U.S. Department of Education 2002.

13. U.S. Department of Education, "Meeting the Highly Qualified Teachers Challenge: The Secretary's Second Annual Report on Teacher Quality" (Washington, D.C., 2003).

14. U.S. Department of Education 2002.

15. Bess Keller, "Rigor Disputed in Standards for Teachers," *Education Week* (January 14, 2004): 1.

16. Diane Ravitch, *Left Back: A Century of Failed School Reforms* (New York: Simon and Schuster, 2000).

17. Terry M. Moe, "Politics, Control, and the Future of School Accountability," in Paul E. Peterson and Martin R. West, eds., *No Child Left Behind? The Politics and Practice of School Accountability* (Washington, D.C.: Brookings Institution, 2003).

18. "Reality Check 2002," *Public Agenda* (New York: 2002). Andrew Rudalevige, "No Child Left Behind: Forging a Congressional Compromise.," in Paul E. Peterson and Martin R. West, eds., *No Child Left Behind.*

19. "The Democratic Contenders," *Education Week* (November 12, 2003).

20. Moe, "Politics, Control, and the Future of School Accountability."

21. General Accounting Office, "No Child Left Behind Act: More Information Would Help States Determine Which Teachers Are Highly Qualified" (Washington, D.C.: General Accounting Office 2003).

22. Ibid., 2–3.

23. Education Trust, "Telling the Whole Truth (or Not) about Highly Qualified Teachers" (Washington, D.C.: Education Trust, 2003a).

24. Ibid., 1.

25. U.S. Department of Education 2003.

26. Keller, "Rigor Disputed," 1.

27. Education Commission of the States, "ECS Report to the Nation" (Denver, Colo., 2004)

28. Christopher O. Tracy and Kate Walsh, "Necessary and Insufficient: Resisting a Full Measure of Teacher Quality" (Washington, D.C.: National Council on Teacher Quality, 2004): 4.

29. Education Commission of the States 2004.

30. Education Trust, "In Need of Improvement: Ten Ways the U.S. Department of Education Has Failed to Live Up to Its Teacher Quality Commitments" (Washington, D.C.: Education Trust, 2003b).

31. Lynn Olson, "Final Rules Give States Direction, Little Flexibility," *Education Week* (December 4, 2002).

32. Education Trust, "Telling the Whole Truth," 2.

33. U.S. Department of Education 2002, 2003.

34. U.S. Department of Education 2003, 5.

35. Frederick Hess, *Tear Down This Wall: The Case for a Radical Overhaul of Teacher Certification* (Washington, D.C.: Progressive Policy Institute, 2001).

Index

academic performance index. *See* API

academic standards, of NCLB, 3, 15, 29–33, 41, 49

accountability, 10–17, 29–30; challenges of, 11–12; consequences relating to, 11, 24, 48, 96; costs of, 53–55; effects of, 53–55; for outcomes, 21; for performance, 48, 96–97; problems with, 12; provisions for, 13, 43; recommendations for, 73–75; rewards relating to, 11; sanctions relating to, 10–17; standards relating to, 59–61; systems of, 10–11. *See also* specific California accountability headings; specific state accountability headings

accountability principles, of NCLB, 4; DOE relating to, 55, 62; improvements due to, 57–59, 58t; NAEP relating to, 57, 95–96, 97–101, 99f, 100f; for performance, 48; sanctions

relating to, 10–17; standard-related requirements of, 56; for states, 29–30; for teachers, 17, 30; testing relating to, 55

achievements; of individual, 17; of school, 14–15, 34n10; of state, 54; of students, 103–5, 111n11

Act tests, 177

adequate yearly progress. *See* AYP

African American students, 54, 67, 96, 100, 101–3, 109–10

Alexander, Lamar, 39

"alignment," 59

America 2000, 48; criticism of, 6; obstacles to, 41–42; standards as part of, 5–6; testing as part of, 5–6, 41

American Educational Research Association, 63

American Federation of Teachers, 20

American Psychological Association, 63

About the Contributors

John E. Chubb, a distinguished visiting fellow at the Hoover Institution, is chief education officer and one of the founders of Edison Schools, a private manager of public schools, including many charter schools. Edison Schools today operates 130 schools in 19 states, with approximately 70,000 students. Chubb is also the coauthor (with task force member Terry M. Moe) of *Politics, Markets, and America's Schools*, a seminal work that argues for the introduction of free market principles within the American education system.

Williamson M. Evers, a research fellow at the Hoover Institution, was senior adviser on education to Ambassador Paul Bremer of the Coalition Provisional Authority in Iraq in 2003. Evers is a member of the White House Commission on Presidential Scholars and was a member of the National Educational Research Policy and Priorities Board in 2001–2002. He serves on panels that write mathematics and history questions for California's statewide testing system and was a commissioner of the California State Commission for the Establishment of Academic Content and Performance. He is coeditor of *School Accountability*, a 2002 publication by the Koret Task Force, and *School Reform: The Critical Issues* and editor of and contributor to *What's Gone Wrong in America's Classrooms*.

Eric A. Hanushek is the Paul and Jean Hanna Senior Fellow at the Hoover Institution. He was nominated by President George W. Bush to be a member of the National Board of Education Sciences. His works on education policy include *Improving America's Schools: The Role of Incentives, Making Schools Work: Improving Performance and Controlling Costs,* and *Educational Performance of the Poor: Lessons from Rural Northeast Brazil.* His current research involves understanding the role of teachers, programs, and funding in determining student achievement. Previously, he served as deputy director of the Congressional Budget Office.

Caroline M. Hoxby, a distinguished visiting fellow at the Hoover Institution, is a professor of economics at Harvard University and director of the Economics of Education Program at the National Bureau of Economic Research. She was nominated by President George W. Bush to serve on the National Board of Education Sciences. She is the editor of *The Economics of School Choice* and the forthcoming book *College Choices.* She is also the author of several influential papers on education policy, including "Does Competition among Public Schools Benefit Students and Taxpayers," "The Effects of Class Size and Composition on Student Achievement: New Evidence from Natural Population Variation," and "Not All School Finance Equalizations Are Created Equal."

Lance T. Izumi is Senior Fellow in California Studies and Director of Education Studies at the San Francisco-based Pacific Research Institute for Public Policy. Izumi is a member of the Board of Governors of the California Community Colleges and a member of the U.S. Department of Education's Teacher Assistance Corps, a task force of teacher-quality experts. He is a past member of the California Postsecondary Education Commission. Izumi is the coeditor of *School Reform: The Critical Issues* (Hoover Institution Press and Pacific Research Institute, 2001) and *Teacher Quality* (Hoover Institution Press and Pacific Research Institute, 2002) and a chapter coauthor for *School Accountability* (Hoover Institution Press, 2002).

Terry M. Moe is a senior fellow at the Hoover Institution and the William Bennett Munro Professor of Political Science at Stanford

University. He is the author of *Schools, Vouchers, and the American Public*, the coauthor (with task force member John E. Chubb) of *Politics, Markets, and America's Schools*, and the editor of *A Primer on America's Schools*. He also edited *Private Vouchers*, the first book to chronicle the growing support for school vouchers for low-income children.

Paul E. Peterson, a senior fellow at the Hoover Institution, is the Henry Lee Shattuck Professor of Government and director of the Program on Education Policy and Governance at Harvard University. He has been appointed to a Department of Education independent review panel to advise in evaluating the Title I program and, in 2003, was awarded the Thomas B. Fordham Foundation prize for Distinguished Scholarship. Peterson is the editor in chief of *Education Next* and author or editor of numerous books on U.S. education, including *No Child Left Behind? The Politics and Practice of School Accountability* (coedited with Martin R. West), *The Future of School Choice, Our Schools and Our Future . . . Are We Still at Risk? The Education Gap: Vouchers and Urban Schools*, and *Earning and Learning: How Schools Matter*.

Diane Ravitch, a distinguished visiting fellow at the Hoover Institution, is a research professor at New York University and holder of the Brown Chair in Education Policy at the Brookings Institution. She is a member of the National Assessment Governing Board, to which she was appointed by Secretary of Education Richard Riley. From 1991 to 1993, she served as assistant secretary of education and counselor to Secretary of Education Lamar Alexander. A historian of American education, she is the author of many books, including *The Language Police: How Pressure Groups Restrict What Students Learn, The Great School Wars, The Troubled Crusade*, and *Left Back: A Century of Failed School Reforms*.

Herbert J. Walberg, a distinguished visiting fellow at the Hoover Institution, is research professor emeritus of education and psychology and University Scholar at the University of Illinois at Chicago. He has edited more than sixty books and written approximately 350 articles on educational productivity and human accomplishment. He was nominated by President George W. Bush to serve on the National Board of Education Sciences and is one of ten U.S. members of the International Academy of Education. He is also a fellow of several scholarly associations in the United States and abroad. He is coauthor of *Education and Capitalism: How Overcoming Our Fear of Markets and Economics Can Improve America's Schools* and coeditor of *School Accountability,* a 2002 publication by the Koret Task Force.

About the Hoover Institution

The Hoover Institution on War, Revolution and Peace, Stanford University, is a public policy research center devoted to advanced study of politics, economics, and political economy "both domestic and foreign" as well as international affairs. With its world-renowned group of scholars and ongoing programs of policy-oriented research, the Hoover Institution puts its accumulated knowledge to work as a prominent contributor to the world marketplace of ideas defining a free society.